**Successful Dr**

Dr Michael Nathenson has been a Senior Lecturer in the Institute of Educational Technology at the Open University since 1974, specialising in the design, development and evaluation of multimedia teaching materials. He has carried out consultancies in Britain, Europe and Asia. Born in Pittsburgh, Pennsylvania, he holds a Ph.D degree in Educational Communications from the Catholic University of America and degrees in Psychology and Social Psychology from the Universities of Wisconsin and Hawaii respectively.

Dr Nathenson is the author of seven books, including *Are You Ready for Your Driving Test?*, also available in Pan Books, and has written widely in the area of multimedia instruction.

Peter Russell is General Secretary and Chief Training Officer of the Driving Instructors' Association. Educated at Leamington College and trained as an educational psychologist, he has since been involved in all aspects of driving, driver training and driver testing. He ran his own driving school for over twenty years, and has held Training Officer positions with the National Joint Council of Approved Driving Instructors' Organisations and the British School of Motoring. He is currently General Secretary and Chief Training Officer of the Motor Schools Association.

Peter Russell broadcasts and writes regularly on driving topics for radio and television and is actively concerned with driver training at international and parliamentary levels.

*Also in Pan Books*
*by Mike Nathenson,*
Are You Ready for Your Driving Test?

# Successful Driving

## Mike Nathenson
## Peter Russell

Illustrations by Brian Folkard
Cartoons by Oliver Preston

**A Pan Original**
**Pan Books** London and Sydney

First published 1986 by Pan Books Ltd
Cavaye Place, London SW10 9PG
9 8 7 6 5 4 3 2 1
© Mike Nathenson 1986
Illustrations © Brian Folkard 1986
Cartoons © Oliver Preston 1986
ISBN 0 330 29206 4
Phototypeset by Input Typesetting Ltd, London SW19 8DR

## Acknowledgements

To Eli, whose love, patience and understanding made the long nights of writing more bearable.

To Zoe, who by the time this book is published will have used it to pass her driving test.

To Sam, Mollie and Donna for their support and encouragement from across the Atlantic.

# Contents

# Introduction

Reading this introduction is your first step towards successful driving – and by successful, I mean

- learning to drive safely and competently
- passing your driving test first time

No book, however, can teach you how to drive a car; this is a skill you need to learn from a good instructor. Nevertheless, this book can make your learning *easier* and help you to become a competent driver much more *quickly*. And, when it is used alongside its companion Pan book *Are You Ready For Your Driving Test?* (which has already helped over 65,000 people to pass their driving tests), your chances of passing the test first time will be greatly increased.

*Successful Driving* takes the new learner through a carefully designed sequence of thirteen stages of driving so he or she can face the driving test without any qualms. Each stage needs to be completed before the next one can be done. For some learners, each stage may be mastered in a single lesson; but for others, some of the stages may require two, three or even more lessons before the learner feels confident to move on. Although your progress depends on many factors (e.g., your age, previous experience, coordination, reflexes, stress level, etc.), you can help yourself best by making absolutely sure that you understand exactly what you have to *know* and *do* in order to satisfy each stage.

The ideal way to gain the most from this book is to choose a professional Approved Driving Instructor (ADI) and use *Successful Driving*:

- to *prepare* yourself for each lesson in advance

- to *supplement* each lesson as you have it, and

- to *reinforce* what you have learned behind the wheel.

Choose your instructor with care and tell him or her that you are using this book to enhance your lessons.

So, before each lesson, prepare yourself by learning exactly what you are going to do. Then, practise it on the road. And finally, after your lesson, read through the stage again to reinforce your learning.

In a nutshell, here is my professional advice for ensuring that you pass your driving test on your first attempt:

1 Choose an Approved Driving Instructor with a proven track record of success.
2 Read each stage of *Successful Driving* before and after each lesson.
3 Do not move on to a new stage until you feel confident that you have mastered the preceding one.
4 When you have mastered all thirteen stages in this book, take the simulated driving test in the bestseller *Are You Ready For Your Driving Test?*
5 Approach the test with confidence, knowing you have had the best tuition possible.

# STAGE 1

# Knowing your car's controls

The easiest way to learn the controls of the car is to remember that they fall into three neat groups:

**Feet**
**Hands**
**Eyes**

It also helps if you realise that none of the controls are difficult to understand or operate. You will find that most of them have much in common with the controls of other things you are used to, like bicycles, sewing machines and other home appliances.

## Foot controls

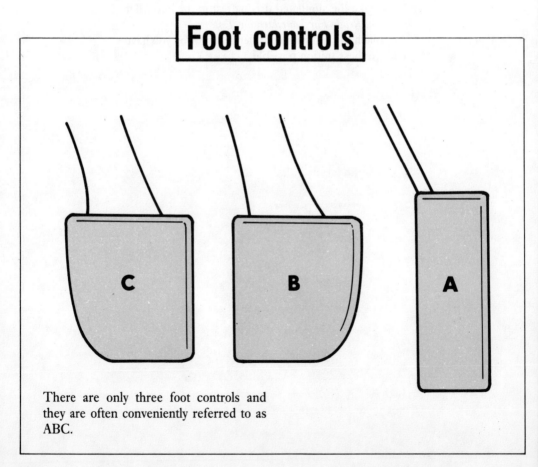

There are only three foot controls and they are often conveniently referred to as ABC.

# Accelerator

The accelerator is the pedal on the far right and is operated by the ball of your foot, using an ankle movement. You can compare the accelerator to the pedals of a bicycle.

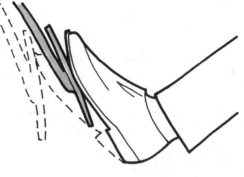

- With the accelerator, the further you push the pedal down, the faster the engine, and therefore the car, goes.

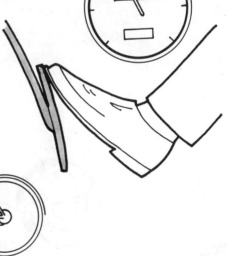

- With the bicycle, the harder you push the pedals around with your feet, the faster the bike goes.

There are, however, three big differences.

1 You don't need any physical effort to make the car move.

2 You only need to use one foot.

3 When you take your right foot off the accelerator pedal, the engine does not stop.

This is very important because it means you can also use your right foot to help control the speed of the car with the next pedal, the footbrake.

# Footbrake

Like the accelerator, the footbrake is also controlled by your right foot, and again an ankle movement is all that is needed.

## Practice

When you first sit in the car, spend a little time practising your right foot movements. Feel the difference between the light return spring of the accelerator pedal and the progressively harder pressure needed on the footbrake.

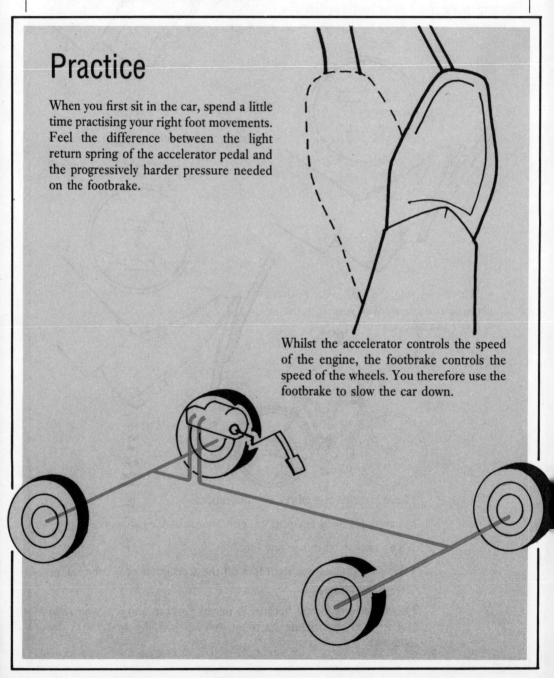

Whilst the accelerator controls the speed of the engine, the footbrake controls the speed of the wheels. You therefore use the footbrake to slow the car down.

You can also slow the car down by decelerating, so that whenever you take your foot off the accelerator pedal, you start to slow the car down.

When you press the brake pedal, you slow the vehicle down even more, by exerting strong pressure on the discs or drums fixed to all four of the wheels.

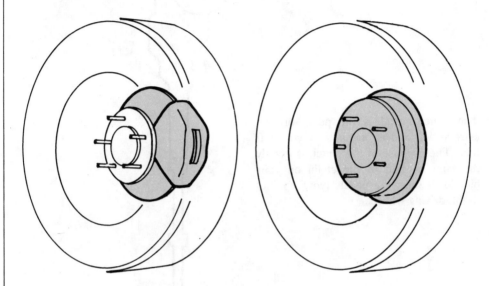

This is exactly the same way that you slow down your bicycle when you use the brakes. But once more, it is made easier for you in the car. On a bicycle, you need to use both hands to operate both brakes together. In a car, your right foot does all the work and the car itself looks after the correct amount of pressure on the front and rear wheels.

### To summarise

- Taking your foot off the accelerator starts to slow you down.
- Putting your foot on the brake continues to slow you down even more.
- Pressing the brake hard enough will stop the car.

# Clutch

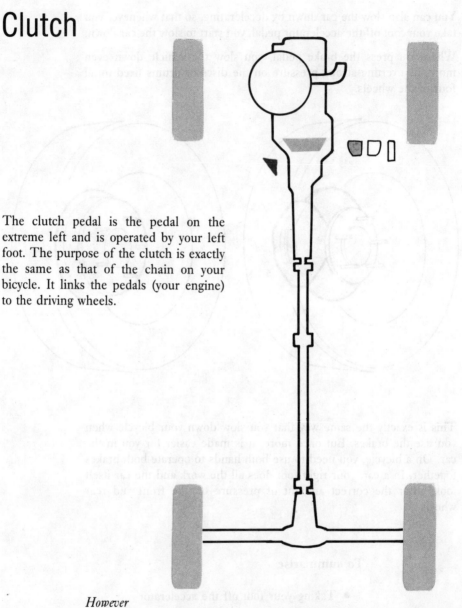

The clutch pedal is the pedal on the extreme left and is operated by your left foot. The purpose of the clutch is exactly the same as that of the chain on your bicycle. It links the pedals (your engine) to the driving wheels.

*However*

- On a bicycle you usually have a 'freewheel' device fitted to enable your feet to have an occasional rest.

- On a car, it suits your purposes better to have a pedal which can join or separate the engine from the wheels, whenever you want to, such as:

    *when you want to stop and start the car

    *when you want to select different gears

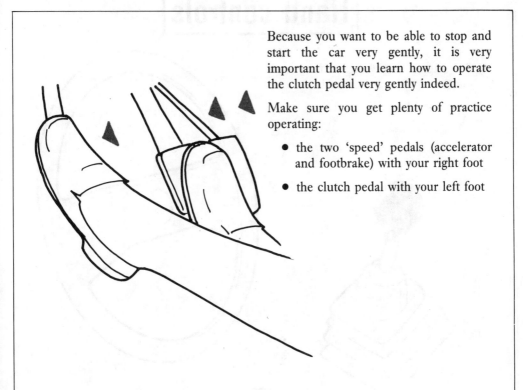

Because you want to be able to stop and start the car very gently, it is very important that you learn how to operate the clutch pedal very gently indeed.

Make sure you get plenty of practice operating:

- the two 'speed' pedals (accelerator and footbrake) with your right foot
- the clutch pedal with your left foot

## Communicating with your instructor

To make your training successful, it is important that you and your instructor agree on the precise wording you will use when you refer to the operation of each of the three pedals. You must be very careful to avoid using misleading or wrong words and also try to be consistent in choosing what words you will use.

- If your instructor says 'A little gas', the meaning is confusing. He could mean a little more gas or a little less gas. However, if he says 'Set the gas' and you agree in advance that that means a certain specific amount of pressure on the pedal, or a certain 'engine noise', then you can say 'More gas' or 'Less gas' and be perfectly clear about what is meant.

- If he says 'Gently brake', you might agree that this means slow down gradually. But 'Gently brake to stop' would mean actually stopping the car. An urgent shout of 'Brake, brake' wouldn't help anyone.

- When using the clutch, you must always remember to listen for the word 'Slowly' before you hear 'Clutch up' so that 'Slowly clutch up' would make sure you apply the gentleness needed.

# Hand controls

At this stage, I only want to concentrate on the three main hand controls.

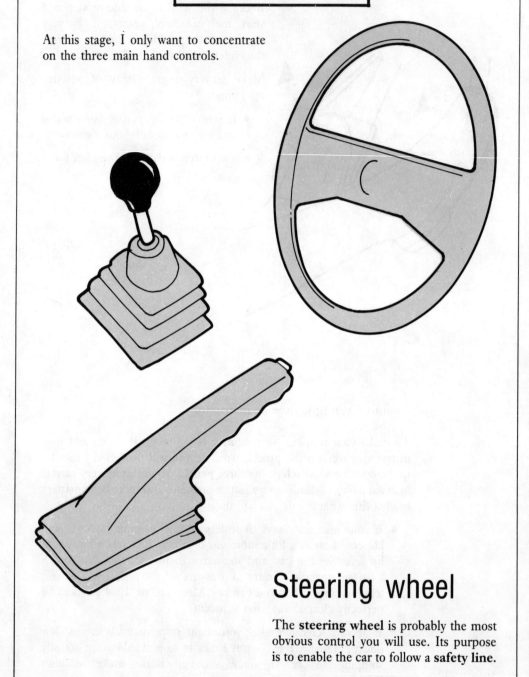

## Steering wheel

The **steering wheel** is probably the most obvious control you will use. Its purpose is to enable the car to follow a **safety line**.

A safety line is the path which you choose
to follow in order to avoid all other traffic.
It is about a door's width from any other
traffic, including both parked or oncoming
cars or other vehicles.

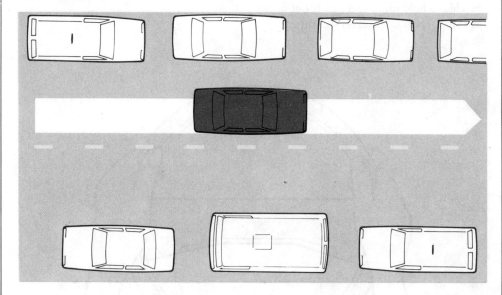

If you find you are unable to maintain a safety line because of
oncoming or parked traffic, you must slow down to give yourself more
time to react. A distance of a door's width, or about one metre, is
adequate at thirty m.p.h. If you only have a narrow gap, like the two
foot clearance in this picture:

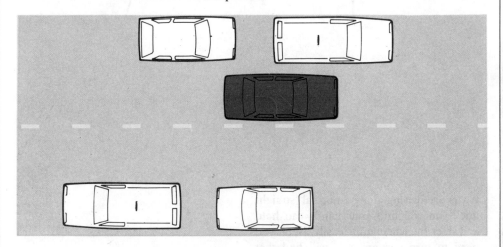

you would be restricted to twenty m.p.h.; and with only one foot, you
must slow down to ten m.p.h.

### Pull-push method of steering

You must always use *both* hands to operate
the steering wheel: and your hands should
be able to hold the wheel lightly but firmly
at **ten-to-two** or **quarter-to-three**.

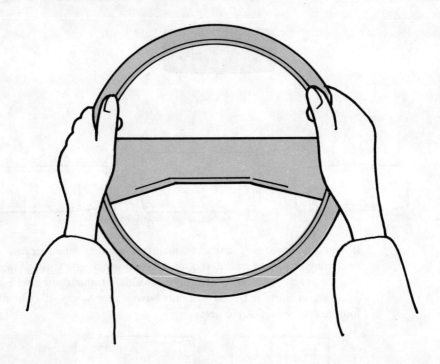

If you are driving along a normal 'straight
line', you will find your hands can hold
and steer the wheel quite easily. But if you
need to turn corners, you will find that
you need to **turn the wheel,** by using a
pull and push movement.

# Practice

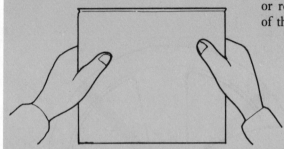

The best way to learn the pull-push method is not in the car at all. Instead you should practise it at home, using a square or rectangular object like a book instead of the wheel.

Move the book in a circular motion by first pulling it down with one hand and then pushing it up with the other. You will soon find that you have to remove the other hand in order to replace it on the wheel at the top.

You will find that there is only *one effective way* to keep the book moving constantly – and that is the way shown in the illustration.

Remember, too, that not only must you feed the wheel when you are turning, but you also need to reverse the process when turning the wheel *back again*.

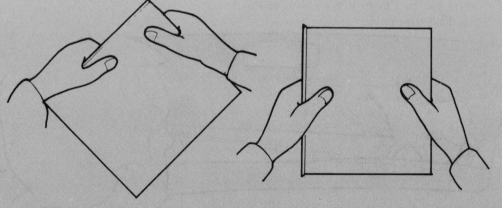

Whenever you have to use any of the other hand controls, like the gear lever, to change gears, it is essential that you return both hands to the correct position on the steering wheel as soon as you can.

Once you learn how to steer and turn the wheel correctly using the pull-push movement, you will never need to cross your hands on the wheel, and you will find that steering soon becomes second nature.

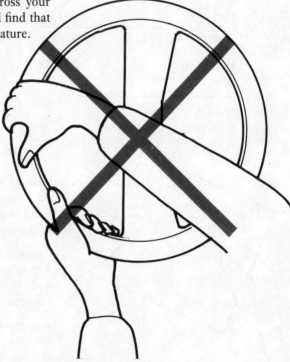

The secret of steering is always to look where you want to go; never look at what you don't want to hit.

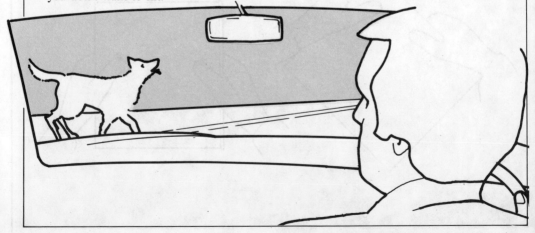

Returning to our bicycle again, it's useful to remember that on a bicycle you also need a 'steering wheel', that is, the handlebars, to maintain your balance. And the steering on a bicycle is direct – a little movement one way or the other can mean a sharp turn.

In a car, you will need to turn the wheel quite a lot to get round a corner.

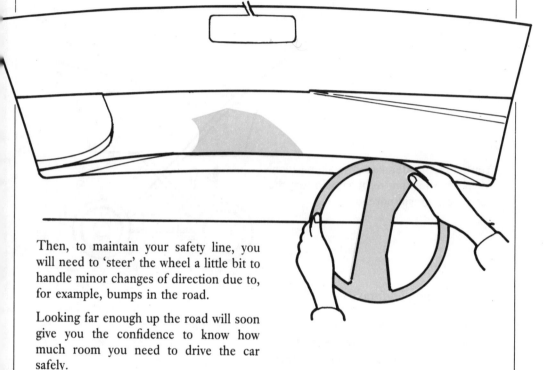

Then, to maintain your safety line, you will need to 'steer' the wheel a little bit to handle minor changes of direction due to, for example, bumps in the road.

Looking far enough up the road will soon give you the confidence to know how much room you need to drive the car safely.

### Three helpful tips

Here are three helpful tips to use on your first few lessons to help you check your position in relation to other cars.

1 Sit in the car at the kerbside and get a feel for the size of your car in relation to other objects on the road.

2 Remember that *your width* is just the same as that of any other car.

3 When you are driving along, look ahead, see how much room the cars in front of you have and remember that you will have the same amount of room too.

# Handbrake

The **handbrake** is sometimes referred to as a parking brake, and if you think of it as a parking brake you will soon get the idea of how and when to use it.

Bicycles don't normally have them, but prams usually do.

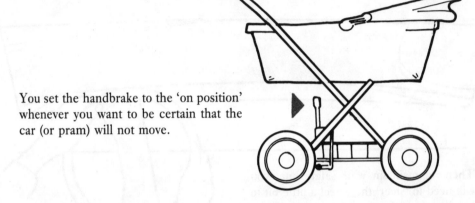

You set the handbrake to the 'on position' whenever you want to be certain that the car (or pram) will not move.

### Applying the handbrake

Whenever your car is stationary, you need to apply either the footbrake or the handbrake. If you stop the car for any length of time, you should use the handbrake. But what is meant by any length of time? And must you always put the handbrake on if you stop the car?

The answers to both of these questions depend on:

- whether the road is flat or on a gradient

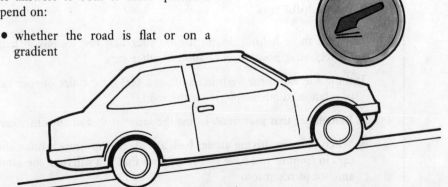

- how long you intend or expect to stop

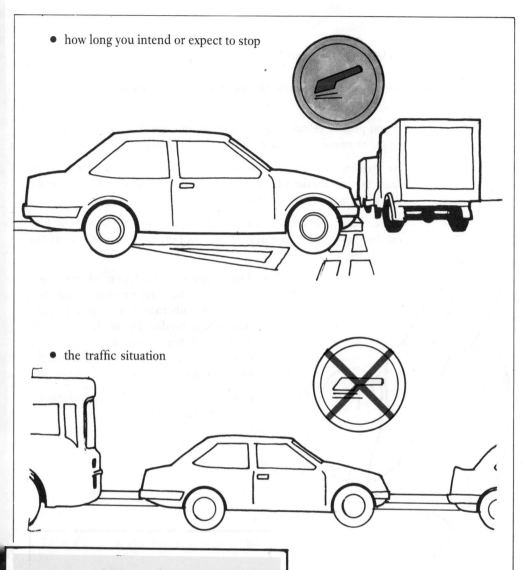

- the traffic situation

**Two guidelines**

There are, however, two guidelines to help you decide.

- If you have time to ask yourself 'Do I need to apply the handbrake?', *you do.*
- If you think you ought to ask yourself 'Should I apply the handbrake?', *you should.*

### Releasing the handbrake

Once you have applied the handbrake, you then need to learn *how* and *when* to release it.

If you plan to release it *as the next movement* with your left hand, you ought to *prepare* to release the handbrake straight away.

By pressing the ratchet with your thumb and by using your hand to hold the handbrake in the applied position, you are giving yourself the advantage of an extra foot.

This means that you can have your foot on the *accelerator,* your foot on the *clutch* and the equivalent of a foot on the *footbrake* – all at the same time.

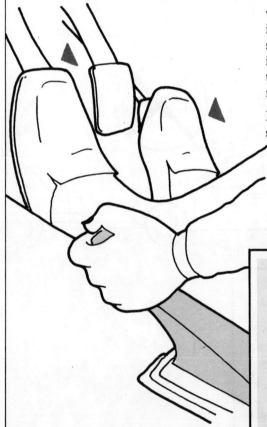

This is an enormous benefit when you are waiting on a hill. But *remember* – don't do it too soon; otherwise it will mean you are sitting there holding the weight of the car in your left hand. And if you get tired, there is the slight danger that the car might roll down the hill.

Releasing the handbrake is a smooth, straightforward movement.

### One helpful tip

If you press the footbrake hard first, this helps to release some of the pressure on the handbrake cable.

This will enable you to press the ratchet button in and release the handbrake smoothly.

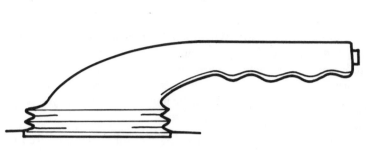

Many cars these days have a warning light which comes on when the handbrake is applied. Always remember to check that the light goes out when you release the brake to make sure that it is completely off.

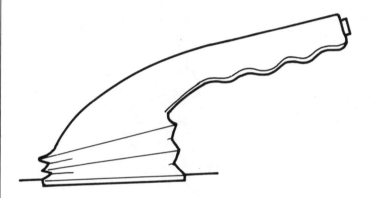

**Five rules about handbrakes**

1 Never pull the brake on by 'clicking it through the ratchet'.

2 Always press the ratchet button in *first*, hold the button down and pull the brake as hard as you can.

3 Move your finger off the button *before* you remove the pressure on the handbrake.

4 Make sure that when you have applied the handbrake the car doesn't move. If it doesn't hold firm, you need to see if there is any more leverage. If there isn't, you may need to have your brakes checked.

5 Never have the handbrake *on* if you are moving at all.

# Gear lever

The last of the hand controls is the **gear lever**, which is simply a device to enable you to select any gear you want without getting your fingers dirty.

Because it is a 'lever', you don't need to exert any pressure on it when you move it forward and backward from gear to gear.

The four gears that we normally find on manual motor cars are intended to make life easy for you when you drive the car.

What you need to remember about the car at all times is that you, the driver, can choose precisely at what speed to travel. In your early driving lessons, you should take all the time you want before you select any new gear.

An easy way for you to think of each of the gears is shown in this illustration.

- First gear is the speed of, say, pushing a pram.

- Third gear is the speed at which a young boy rides his bike.

- Second gear is the speed of a vicar riding his bicycle.

- Fourth gear is an ordinary car speed.

**When to use the four gears:**

- First gear, the lowest, is the gear you use to start off and drive slowly.

- Second gear, slightly faster, is the gear you would choose to drive round most corners.

- Third gear takes you into faster-moving traffic and would be the gear you choose quite a lot during your early lessons. Third is a useful gear for giving you time to make decisions and, as such, is usually very flexible. By flexible, I mean that it will let you drive from about eight m.p.h. at the low end, up to about fifty m.p.h.-plus at the top end.

- Fourth gear, or top gear, is the least powerful, but it does give you the widest range of speeds. It is the most common gear to use for normal driving and when on dual carriageways and motorways.

- Fifth gear or overdrive: some cars have a fifth gear or an 'overdrive' fitted, which has the effect of giving extra gears. In all cases overdrive is intended to enable the driver to use a very high gear to conserve fuel. Overdrive is only used at higher speeds when the car is cruising along without any strain.

## Selecting gears

The gear lever comes up through the floor and the gears are selected in the form of a figure H.

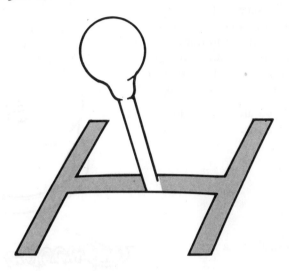

You only need light pressure to move the gear lever. From this illustration, you can see that:

- by pressing lightly to the left and forward, you will select first

- by pressing to the left and backwards, you will select second

- by pulling to the right and forward, you will select third

- by pulling to the right and backwards, you select fourth

### Don't worry about gears

Many learner drivers worry about gears and some people suggest they learn to drive in automatic cars to make life easier. But it is no more difficult to learn which gear to use than it is to learn in which saucepan to boil an egg or which size knitting needle to use to knit a wool jumper.

- If the one you are using is too big, use a smaller one.

- If it is too small, try a larger one.

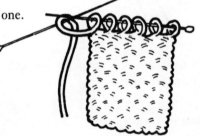

# Practice

A useful way to practise using the gear lever is to sit in the car and place your hand *around* the gear lever in such a way that you cup it with your hand.

Hold it one way, then the other, to practise moving it from one gear, through neutral, to the next gear. When you have had a few driving lessons, you will soon find that smooth gear changing depends upon getting a simple sequence off pat.

# Eye controls

Let's now move on to the
third group of controls – the
**eye controls**.

# Windscreen

The windscreen gives you a clear picture of the road ahead; it's your
responsibility to keep it clean and clear.

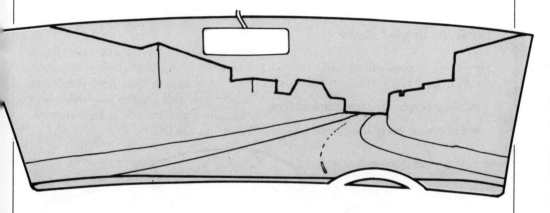

Always sit in a position that allows you to see as far up the road as
possible.

# Rear view mirrors

When you need to know what is happening behind you, and you'll
need to do this a lot, you'll have to look through the rear view mirrors.
There is always one in the middle of your windscreen and quite often
you will find you have one or two other mirrors fitted on the doors
or wings of the car.

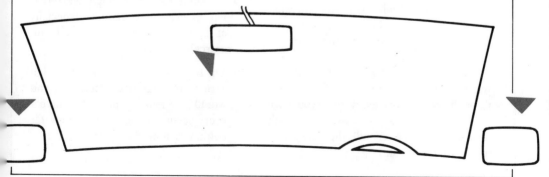

Some people refer to the mirror in a motor car as the 'third eye' and, certainly, this is a very good way in which to think of it.

Your eyes should always be scanning the road ahead all the time to see what information you can gather about things you will need to react to.

But you also need to be aware of what is coming up *behind* you, especially faster-moving traffic. A car which always stays thirty or forty metres behind you is no problem. You are aware of his presence and you both know that, whatever hazard you meet, he is likely to meet the same hazard soon after you.

The most important use of the mirror is to warn you about cars or vans coming from behind you, which may want to overtake you.

### The secret of good mirror use

The secret of good mirror use is to take checks behind you at frequent intervals:

- Some people say every hundred feet.

- Others say every five seconds.

*But both are wrong.* No one can tell you how often you need to check your mirror; you simply have to know what is going on behind you and whether the situation is changing – and *you need to know instantly,* before it's too late.

While you are driving, your mind should carry a picture of what is ahead and what is behind. Your eyes tell you all the time how the pattern ahead is changing, so you can update the information immediately. But with the changing traffic behind you, you must make a conscious effort to look through the mirrors every time you have the opportunity, just to convince yourself that the situation is still the same and under your control.

- On some roads, you might leave it as late as every ten seconds, especially at night, on a long straight road with scarcely any traffic.

- On other busy roads, like the High Street on a Saturday afternoon, you would be looking in your mirrors every second to see exactly how far behind or how close a certain car is.

## Mirrors are deceptive

Your mirrors do not always tell you the truth. They often tell you what is behind you – provided whatever it is keeps up a constant speed and position. That way you know exactly how close it is, and what it is doing.

But some mirrors give a more distorted picture than others. This applies especially to **curved or concave mirrors,** usually fitted on the outside of the car. As you can see from this picture, they give you a wider angle of vision, but make things look further away.

The **convex** mirror fitted to the inside middle of your windscreen gives a narrow angle of vision and makes things look closer.

### Three rules about your mirrors

1 Always inspect your mirrors carefully.

2 Make sure you know what type of mirror you have and what angle of vision it gives you.

3 Compare the picture and size you see in the door wing mirror with the inside mirror and by looking behind.

### An exercise in observation

Now here's a simple exercise in observation for you to do while sitting in your car.

# Practice

- Stay in the driving seat.

- Ask your passenger or someone else to walk all round the car – very slowly – and to stop each time you see them disappear or partly disappear from view.

- You will find this especially noticeable at each of the pillars of the car's windows.

- There are six of them normally and they are called the six **blind spots** in which you could find danger lurking.

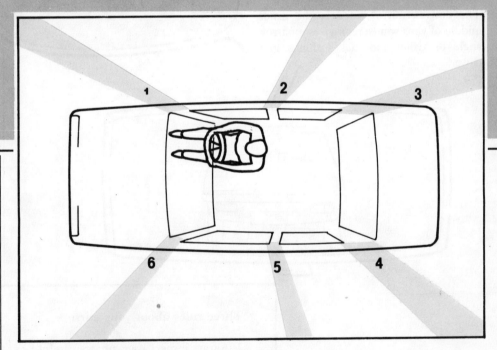

### Dangerous blind spots

Each of these six blind spots represents potential danger.

- It might be a cyclist overtaking you on the right while you are stopped and about to open your door.

- Or it might be a child crossing the road, just out of sight of your side mirror.

- Or it might even be a motor cycle policeman coming up on your left.

### When to check your blind spots

The most important time to check your blind spot is when you are about to move away from the side of the road.

1 First, check the road ahead to see if it seems clear.

2 Then, look through the inside and side mirrors to see if it all seems safe.

3 Finally, give that little life-saver look over your right shoulder to see if that overtaking cyclist is in that one position which guarantees that you cannot see him in your mirrors.

If you ever need to move left from a position out from the kerb, you must also check the blind spot on the *left*, in case a motorcyclist or cyclist should sneak up on the inside of you. This often applies when you are turning left, say at traffic lights, and you are in a slow-moving stream of traffic. A good look to the left will soon show if there are any hidden dangers.

### One final tip

If you are waiting to move away from the side of the road into a busy road, the fact that you look over your right shoulder at your right-hand blind spot tells any driver approaching you that you have seen him. You are then much less likely to pull out in front of the other driver.

Just think how pleased you are when you see someone looking round at you. The problem with mirrors is that it is so easy to lose eye contact with other road users.

# Minor controls

Hopefully, you now understand how all the main controls work. You now need to make sure you understand the position and operation of the more important of the **minor controls.**

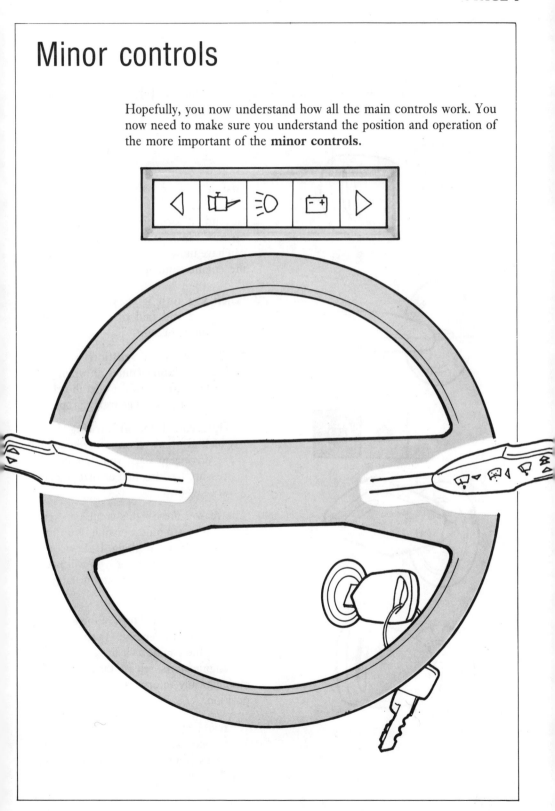

### Ignition key: four stages

You insert the **ignition key** into the lock and, by turning it slowly, you will feel it go through the four stages:

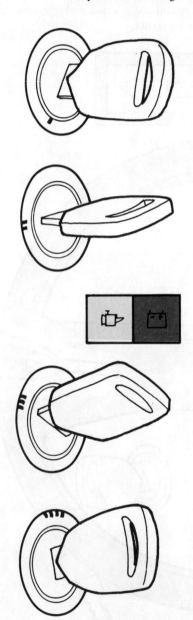

1 First, it unlocks the steering wheel.

2 Second, it switches on the **auxiliary circuit** which simply means that you can have things like the radio on without the engine running.

3 When you turn it again to the third notch, you will find that two warning lights will come on.

- The first is the **ignition warning light** which only comes on when you are driving to warn you that the electrical system is not charging properly.

- The second is the **oil warning light,** which also only comes on when you are driving to warn you that the oil pressure has dropped or that you are very low on oil.

The reason these lights come on every time you switch on the engine is to show you that they are working. If they come on while you are driving, you will need to pull in and check what the fault is before continuing.

4 The fourth and final turn of the ignition key will start the engine. Turn the key, listen to the engine as it fires and, when the engine starts, release the key, which automatically returns it to the previous position.

*Never switch off the ignition* while you are driving, because it locks the steering wheel. This is a very dangerous situation, to say the least.

## Indicator switch

Probably the most used of all the minor controls is the **indicator switch**. This is usually a stalk that sticks out at the side of the wheel. The idea behind this and all stalk switches is that they can be operated without removing your hand from the wheel.

The indicator stalk is typical. You will find that it moves up or down in the same direction the wheel turns (clockwise or anti-clockwise) so that you move it left or right with the wheel. It is normally turned off or cancelled automatically by the steering wheel as the wheel turns back to the straight-ahead position.

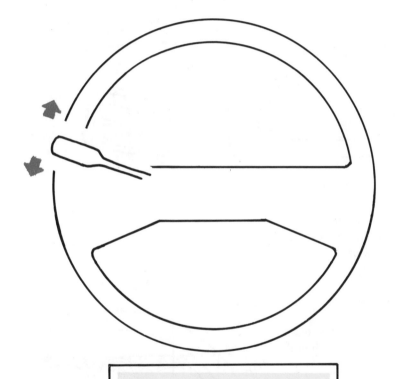

### Two rules for indicators

1 Make sure that you signal the correct direction.

2 Make sure that the indicator switch is cancelled as soon as you do not need the signal any longer.

## A warning

There is another warning to be borne in mind about this switch. On most cars the stalk containing the indicator also operates other signals. For example, on some cars you press it in to sound the horn and you pull it towards you to flash the headlamps.

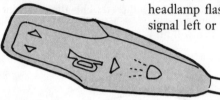

*Take great care* when you learn to use this control to ensure that you don't give headlamp flashes when you only mean to signal left or right.

## Windscreen wiper switch

The **windscreen wiper switch** is often found on the other side of the wheel to the indicator stalk.

It, too, operates a number of items, like the two-speed wipers and the screen washers.

Ask your instructor to go through each of these controls in turn to make sure you don't confuse wipers with signals, or give other drivers the wrong signal.

## Other minor controls

You will also need to find out, identify and learn how to operate each of the following minor controls:

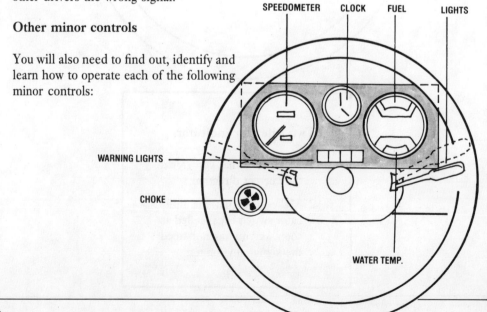

# Seating position

In the early days of learning to drive, you must make sure you are sitting in a relaxed position in the car. The first time you ever sit behind the controls you may find the prospect daunting, but you can soon overcome your fear when you realise that it's easier to sit comfortably in a car than it is to sit on a bicycle. In fact, even the act of driving a car is easier than controlling a bicycle.

Ideally, you should be sitting square in the seat with your bottom firmly pressed into the seat and backrest. In this illustration, the learner is sitting in the *correct* position. He can push all three pedals right down to the floor without moving his body forward and, at the same time, he can hold the steering wheel lightly but firmly.

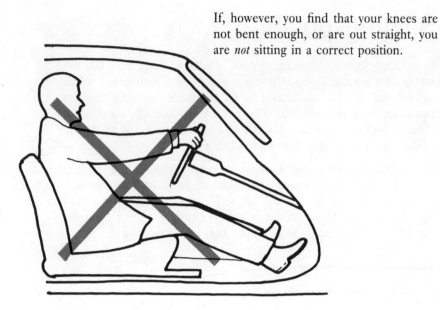

If, however, you find that your knees are not bent enough, or are out straight, you are *not* sitting in a correct position.

You will probably need to adjust your seat forward to get a more comfortable position. This will enable you to operate the controls with confidence.

Get your instructor to show you how to adjust your particular seat, find out your own special requirements and make sure you can recognise them each time you get into the car.

### Three final points about seat adjustments

1 Once you have moved the seat, *make sure it is locked in place.* If you don't, there's the danger that it might slide back so far that you won't reach the brake when you need to.

2 If you have trouble seeing over the top of the steering wheel, you'll need to use a cushion to raise you up unless your car has a height and slope adjustment for the seat.

3 If you do use a cushion, make sure it is securely fastened to the seat so that it can't slide around.

# STAGE 2

# Signalling, braking and changing gear

## Signalling correctly

When you were a child, you probably found that your mother didn't mind where you went or what you did, within reason, as long as she knew what you were doing *before* you did it. The same rule still applies to your driving lessons, except that you are not concerned so much about your mother as about other road users. The most important road user whom you have to tell anything to is the one who is driving behind you.

A signal is only useful to other road users if it can be seen and understood early enough for them to take any necessary action to avoid you.

The purpose of a signal is to communicate your intentions. As such, it forms an important part of your driving pattern:

- First, decide what you want to do.

- Then, check your mirrors.

- Next, look to see who might need to know what you intend to do.

- Finally, tell them clearly, and in good time, so that they won't be taken by surprise when you change speed or direction.

The signals you give need to be clear and unmistakable. Most of them are fairly obvious.

The most frequent signals you'll be giving when you drive are the amber indicators, which are at the front and back of most cars.

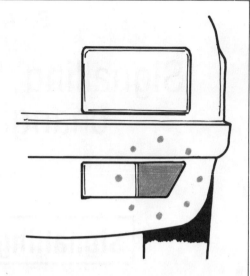

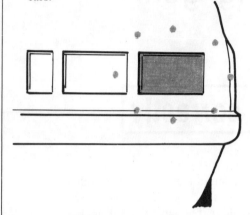

The way the indicators move is almost always the same way as the steering wheel turns. This is to enable the signal to be cancelled by the steering wheel as it returns to the straight-ahead position.

There will be times when the self-cancelling mechanism does *not* work, and that means you have to make certain that you check they do cancel every time.

You, as the driver, are totally responsible for every aspect of signalling, and, above all, for making every signalling decision a thoughtful act.

- Having checked your mirrors, decide at what point to give the signal.

- Make absolutely sure there is no danger of the signal being misinterpreted by anyone else.

- Having decided when to start the signal, remember how long to continue it; this especially applies to passing and overtaking other traffic.

- Make sure the signal is cancelled immediately after its usefulness is over.

# Which signal to use

Another important decision you need to make is *which* signal to use.

The signals you give are simple: I intend to *turn left*, or *turn right* or *slow down*.

- If you intend to move out or turn to the *right*, you will normally use the right-flashing indicator.

- If you intend to move out or turn to the *left*, you will use the left indicator.

- If you intend to slow down, you could use your brake lights, which come on automatically each time you press the brake pedal.

But the problem with brake lights to tell people you are slowing down is, of course, that they only operate *when* you slow down – a bit too late.

So, at such times, you must also use an **arm signal** to say you are intending to slow down.

### Arm signals

Notice the word 'arm'. This is to stress the need to put the length of your arm out of the window if you intend to signal in this way. A 'hand' signal wouldn't be noticed.

Here are the three signals you would give by arm:

**1** turning or moving out to the right

**2** turning or moving out to the left

3 slowing down or stopping

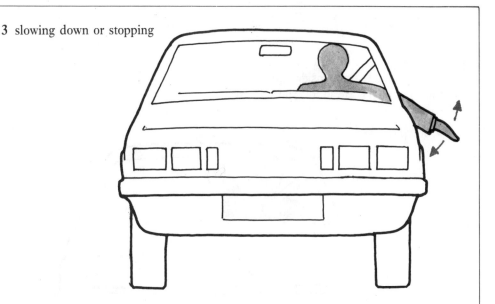

When you give a slowing-down arm signal:

- put your arm out of the window

- move it up and down as shown in the third illustration above

- say to yourself, 'I am slowing down, I am slowing down' before you bring it back in.

- don't keep it out any longer than necessary (many drivers suffer from the terminal disease of steering without any hands on the wheel)

There are five other advantages of using a slowing-down signal by arm, apart from the obvious one of being able to do it before you begin to slow down.

1 It draws attention to itself because it is unusual.

2 You can warn people in front as well as behind you.

3 It benefits the traffic immediately behind you (and sometimes three or four cars back in the queue, too) when given *before* you actually touch the brake lights

4 It benefits a pedestrian waiting at a crossing.

5 It benefits a bus waiting to move off.

There are two extra things you need to remember about arm signals.

1 You need to make them very clear and distinct.

2 They can't always be easily seen by all other traffic.

## Signals by hand

Occasionally, you will also need to give signals by 'hand' from inside the car to traffic controllers ahead of you. These signals are:

- going straight on

- turning left

- turning right

You must make sure that the person to whom you are signalling can see the signal you are giving. This especially applies to cars with deep windscreens.

Make sure your hand can actually be seen easily and look out for the same signals being given to you by other road users.

### Misinterpreting signals

There is a danger of misinterpreting signals. For example, when you intend to pull in and stop, many drivers often use the left-turn signal without thinking what it could mean.

> **A B C of arm and hand signals**
>
> - Make sure they **Aid** other road users.
> - Keep them **Brief** and unambiguous.
> - Make them **Clear.**

Quite often you will see a driver signal left and people follow him, assuming he intends to make the next left turn.

This often causes the following car to have to take a sharp, avoiding action when the correct meaning is realised. So, if you think your signal to pull in might be misread, it is better to give an arm signal.

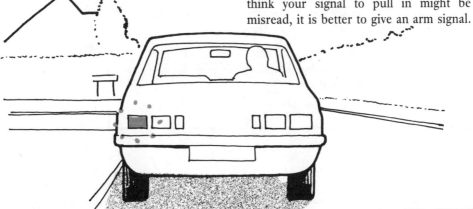

### Horns and flashers

You can also signal your presence to other road users by using the horn and headlamp flashers. But you must never use these as a way of telling other people what you want them to do; for example, flashing your headlamps to tell another car that he can turn a corner in front of you, or tooting your horn to tell another driver you don't approve of one of his actions.

*The Highway Code* is quite explicit on the use of the horn and flashers. Their only purpose is to draw attention to the fact that you are there. Don't use them for any other purpose.

### To summarise

Signalling requires a lot of thought and intelligent signalling makes you and the roads safer.

### Five steps to correct signalling

1 Decide which signal to use and how you will give it.

2 Signal early and decisively.

3 Make sure your signal is seen by all road users who need to know of your intentions.

4 Decide if you need to give a second or supplementary signal like, perhaps, an arm signal to reinforce the indicator and to say you are moving out *and* turning right in close succession.

5 Make sure you have cancelled your signal immediately after it is no longer required.

Here are three common questions and answers often asked about signalling.

**1 Should I give both an arm signal and an indicator?**
Not normally, but there are exceptions; for instance, when you are moving away from the kerb and then intending to turn right immediately afterwards. Or if you intend to stop on the right, when there are also right turns.

**2 Should I use a slowing-down signal with indicators?**
No. The signal to turn left or right also means you would expect to slow down to start the turn.

**3 When should I signal, or when can I not bother to signal?**
You should always signal your intentions if there is anyone around who needs to know them. If you *know* that no one can see them and that no one could possibly benefit, you can omit the signal. But if you have any doubt, it is always better to signal.

# Braking properly

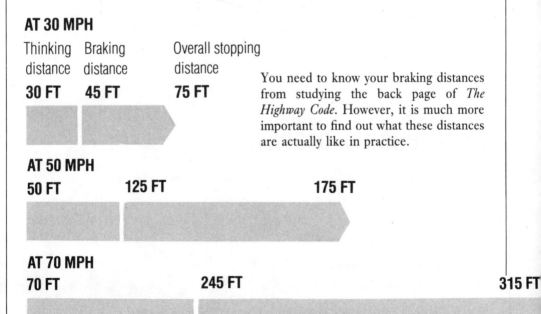

**AT 30 MPH**

| Thinking distance | Braking distance | Overall stopping distance |
|---|---|---|
| 30 FT | 45 FT | 75 FT |

You need to know your braking distances from studying the back page of *The Highway Code*. However, it is much more important to find out what these distances are actually like in practice.

**AT 50 MPH**

50 FT        125 FT                175 FT

**AT 70 MPH**

70 FT              245 FT                    315 FT

Braking firmly and positively has the effect of changing the stability of the car. Also, all the weight of the car is thrown over the front wheels. This is a pity, because you also use your front wheels to steer.

Because braking affects the way the car will steer, you have an important rule to remember:

**One basic rule about braking**

Never brake and turn the steering wheel at the same time.

The secret is to do the braking first; then you have rolling wheels to steer the car through the safety line.

# Mirror, signal, manoeuvre

The sequence of **mirror, signal, manoeuvre** or MSM emphasises the fact that braking is part of the manoeuvre, so early planning is essential. The secret is to be looking far enough ahead so that you are not taken by surprise. Plan your driving so that your braking is always smooth and the result of a planned sequence of actions.

# Progressive braking

Whenever you meet a hazard which requires you to slow down or stop:

- check your mirrors
- give any necessary signal
- come off the accelerator
- cover the brake pedal
- if this does not slow you down enough, press down on the brake pedal in order to arrive at the speed you need

As with so many things connected with learning to drive, the earlier this sequence is done, the more time you have to react.

Ideally, you should try to brake gradually and smoothly with light pressure at first over a reasonably long distance and then gradually increase the pressure as it is needed – *progressively* is the right way to slow down.

Progressive braking begins the moment your right foot comes off the accelerator, which slows down the engine and automatically has a braking effect on the car.

# The clutch and skids

It is important to remember that correct braking does not require you to press down the clutch pedal. The secret is to choose the speed you require first and then select the gear most suited to that speed when you have reached it.

If you were to press the clutch down at the same time as you take your foot off the accelerator, you would lose that important deceleration. And in so doing, you could seriously risk a skid.

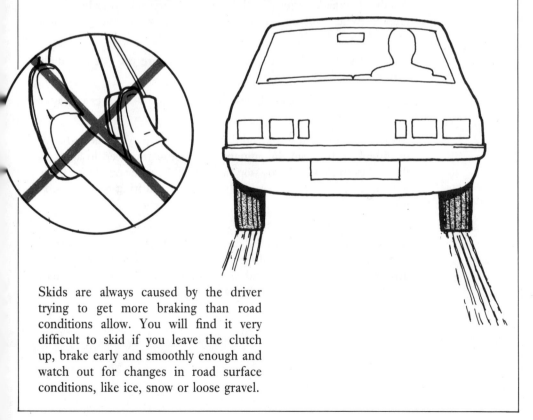

Skids are always caused by the driver trying to get more braking than road conditions allow. You will find it very difficult to skid if you leave the clutch up, brake early and smoothly enough and watch out for changes in road surface conditions, like ice, snow or loose gravel.

# Stopping

Always plan your driving far enough ahead so that you know exactly where you intend to stop; you will then find that you can almost release the pressure on the brakes just before this point and you will be able to stop without jerking.

You should think of stopping as 'bringing the car to rest'. To slow the car from thirty m.p.h. to twenty-five m.p.h., you do not need much brake pressure; similarly, to bring the car to rest from five m.p.h. only requires light pressure.

The hallmark of the skilled driver is the ability to bring the car to rest without the passenger being aware of it.

Having stopped, you now need to ensure that the car doesn't move until you want it to. So you may well have to keep the brake pedal pressed firmly, or you may need to apply the handbrake. This is especially true on hills, of course; but you must also remember to apply the brakes when you are on the level.

# Check your brakes

Another hallmark of the skilled driver is to never take your brakes for granted. Whenever you get into a car, any car, you should always test the brakes.

1 First, try the brake pedal to see what pressure you need to apply to make it work.

2 Then, test the brakes themselves – as soon as you can – after moving off.

Remember, too, that when you drive different cars you will find a lot of difference between the amount of pressure you need to apply to the brakes to slow down or stop the car. Make sure you always know how much pressure the particular car you are driving needs to stop it.

When you get used to driving just one car, your own, you must remember that your brakes will wear out. It is therefore very important that you have them checked frequently. One way is to ask a friend to drive your car occasionally and to tell you if he notices that the brakes are not operating as well as they were the last time he drove the car.

## A braking checklist

When braking, you should pay particular attention to the following items.

- Your own reaction time.
- The condition of your car – especially the brakes, steering and suspension.
- The condition and type of tyres fitted.
- The size and weight of the car, as well as the load you may be carrying.
- The gradient of the road and any camber.
- The weather and visibility.
- The road condition and, in particular, the surface of the road and what sort of grip your tyres will have at any given time.

## The 'do nots' of braking

- **Do not** brake on bends or curves.
- **Do not** start to brake too late.
- **Do not** take your foot off the brake in order to change gear (especially downhill).
- **Do not** brake fiercely as you bring the car to rest.
- **Do not** release the footbrake before the handbrake has been applied.
- **Do not** forget to take the weather and road surface into account before braking.
- **Do not** forget to allow for extra weight in your car, or the steepness of hills, before braking.
- **Do not** forget to test your brakes, whenever you drive, before you need them.

# Changing gears

Most learner drivers dread the thought of gear-changing, mainly because they are sitting in a motor car, and all they can see is a long lever sticking up through the floor boards, or sometimes sticking out from the dashboard or even on the side of the steering wheel.

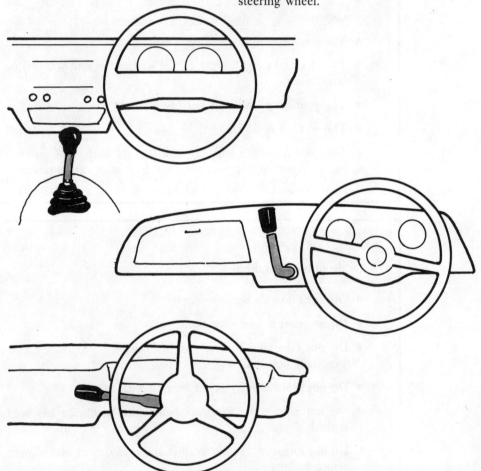

They have no idea what is stuck on the other side of the lever.

To change gears correctly, you need to learn two skills.

- *How* to change gears.
- *When* to change gears.

Both of these skills really depend upon knowing *why* you need to change gears.

The answer is to keep the car comfortable.

Imagine riding a bicycle which has gears.

- If you pedal uphill, you will find that you get slower and slower.

- If you can change to a lower gear, you will find that by pedalling faster (although the bike travels just as slowly as before) it is much easier to pedal.

- If you slip into high gear when you are going faster, you will find that you can pedal more slowly (although the bike keeps going quite quickly).

The gearbox in the car works exactly the same as the separate cogs on a bicycle's gears. You merely select a gear which enables the engine to purr along at a nice even speed, while letting the back wheels travel at whatever speed is most suited to the road and traffic conditions (and, of course, at the speed which you select).

# Selecting the four gears

With a normal car, you have four gears.

- **First gear** is the lowest, slowest and most powerful. This is the gear which you use for starting the car from rest.

- **Second gear** enables you to build up your speed. It is also the gear you would use when you want to go slow enough to turn a corner, but not stop altogether.

- **Third gear** is probably the most useful gear that you have; it covers most things you will need to do in a motor car. It's also a very good gear for coping with problems. If, for example, you're driving along the road and see something up ahead and you are not sure how best to cope with it, third gear will often solve the problem by giving you *time* to work the situation out.

- **Fourth gear,** in most cars, is usually the last one you can select and is the gear you choose for normal driving in ordinary traffic.

In fact, fourth gear is not actually a gear at all. Let's see why.

The gearbox of a motor car is a big box between the engine and the driving wheels. Inside it, a whole lot of cogs and wheels with teeth on them are joined together to reduce the engine speed from (say) 2000 turns per minute to a more *reasonable* 500 or 1000 turns or so.

Although this is how the gearbox actually works, when you are in fourth gear, you actually miss out the gearbox completely. So the car is at its most comfortable when you are in fourth gear, and this takes all the strain away from the box with the gears in them.

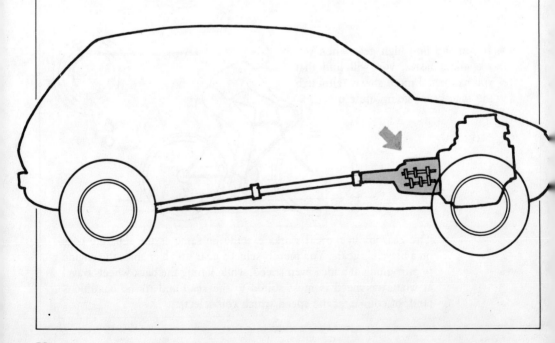

# Changing gears

As a new driver, you choose the speed at which you want to travel and the speed at which you feel safest – and both of these will determine which gear you should be in at any particular moment.

We looked at *how* you change gears in Stage 1, 'Knowing your car's controls'. Always remember that the purpose of any lever is to transfer 'energy' from one object to another and, in this case, it is energy from your hand to the gears in the box. So you never need to put any weight into the effort of selecting a gear.

A gentle movement is all that is needed, with your hand pressing the gear lever in one of two directions: across to the left or right and forward or backward.

# Gear-changing sequence

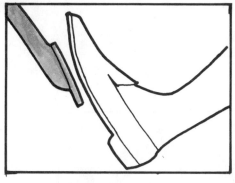

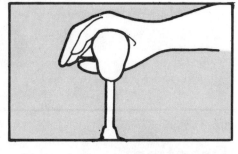

1 Cover the clutch.

2 Place your hand on the gear lever with your palm towards the instructor (for first and second).

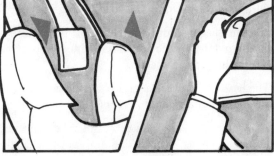

3 Press the clutch down and select a gear from the one it is in – through the neutral position – to the new gear.

4 *Slowly* allow the clutch to come up and press down the accelerator.

5 Move your hand back to the steering wheel.

When changing up, if you do it *early* enough, you will find that the bottom end of each gear is about the same road speed as the top end of the previous gear.

Changing gear *down* is no more difficult than changing *up*. But you will have to try extra hard to learn to 'listen' to the engine noise to make sure that, when your clutch is *slowly* let up, you let the accelerator pedal increase the engine speed to suit the road speed in the new gear.

There are two important things to remember about changing gears:

1 You do not have to select each gear in turn, if you are slowing down. Sometimes you will find that plenty of braking will enable you to miss out one or more of the gears completely.

2 You *always* choose what speed you want to drive at and *then* select the best gear for that speed.

# Practice

Get plenty of gear-changing practice on nice quiet 'practice' roads, starting in first, moving off, picking up enough speed for second, then third, and fourth too if the road is long enough.

Practise slowing down by changing down through the gears from fourth to third to second and back into first once more, crawling along at a pushing-pram speed.

The best way to practise gear changing is when you are also practising turning left and right at corners.

Find yourself a nice square set of roads and get plenty of practice starting, moving off, picking up speed, changing gears and then slowing down in order to turn the next corner.

## Changing down to go faster

On rare occasions during your lessons you will find it is necessary to change down to a lower gear *in order to go faster*. This is most likely to happen when you find that the car is struggling a little bit. Because you need extra 'power', you will need to change down to a lower gear in order to get it.

You obviously do not want to lose any more speed than necessary while you are changing down; so what you have to do is to change from (say) fourth gear to third, at about thirty m.p.h. Because your engine speed will need to rise to meet the needs of third gear at thirty m.p.h., you should keep your foot on the accelerator as you make the change. You do not need to increase the engine speed a lot and experience will tell you just how much. This will mean you are travelling at the same speed as before, but with much more power available to help you to overtake or climb a steep hill.

## Changing gears: early lessons

Practice and understanding are vitally important to the whole art of changing gears. In your early lessons, you will find that you need to change gear at the lower end of the speed scale:

| | |
|---|---|
| First | 0–5 m.p.h. |
| Second | 3–10 m.p.h. |
| Third | 8–25 m.p.h. |
| Fourth | 20–30+ m.p.h. |

## Changing gears: last lessons

But when you are nearer the end of your lessons, you will find that you can often take advantage of the power build-up of the gears to stay in them longer in order to pick up speed more quickly. Your gear/speed range will then look more like this scale:

| | |
|---|---|
| First | 0–10 m.p.h. |
| Second | 8–25 m.p.h. |
| Third | 22–50 m.p.h. |
| Fourth | 50–70 m.p.h. |

Although you are still using the same gears, you are now simply taking advantage of the flexibility of the gears to enable you to make better use of the power of the car.

It doesn't take very long for a good learner driver to recognise the times when it is useful to hang on to lower gears for more power; at that point, you become your own 'automatic' gear selector.

# Driving an automatic car

Many learner drivers wonder if some learning problems would be solved, or at least reduced, if they were to learn to drive an automatic car instead of a geared car.

For most people, the reasoning behind the thought is the fear that there are so many mechanical things to do in a motor car that they will never remember – or master them all – in the time they have set themselves to learn to drive.

They often ask 'If I can forget all about gears and clutches, will it be easier for me to drive?'

Although the answer is yes, the actual difference in the number of lessons required is not as great as you first think. The reason is that the bulk of lessons you take is not spent on learning to control a motor car, but on learning to control the road traffic situation around you – and this requires the same number of lessons whether the car is automatic or geared.

If you concentrate on the way that the clutch and gears *help* you to gain full control of the car easily and fairly quickly, you will soon be able to drive the geared car 'automatically' anyway.

But what if you really want to learn to drive on an automatic?

There are, of course, three real benefits, especially in the early lessons.

1 You will be able to appreciate the first benefit immediately as you find yourself sitting behind the wheel of the automatic car. You will be delighted to find that you only have two pedals, the accelerator and the footbrake, to master, not three.

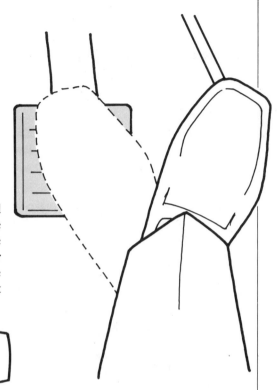

But strange as it might seem, you still only use your right foot. This is because the basic rules about the speed of the engine still apply to automatics. Your right foot controls the speed of the engine and the wheels and your left foot stays out of sight.

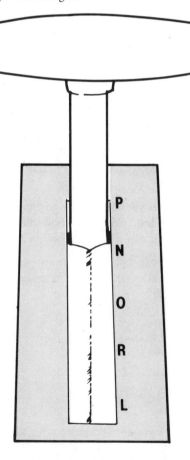

2 The second benefit has to do with the gear lever on the automatic, which looks different from a geared car. Instead of first, second, third, fourth and neutral, the automatic is usually marked P (for Park), N (for Neutral) and D (for Drive).

Because there is no clutch the car is automatically ready to move off. (You do not need to 'synchronise' the clutch and accelerator pedals like you do on a geared car).

3 The third important benefit is that it automatically selects the correct gear for the job which the car is expected to do.

If your engine speed drops too low, it will automatically select the correct lower gear.

If your engine speed rises, it will automatically select a higher gear.

### Three extra tricks

There are three extra tricks you will need to learn about automatics:

1 How to hold the car in a low gear in certain circumstances, like driving down a very steep hill, to prevent the car from selecting its own gear.

2 How to use 'kickdown' (a way of kicking down the accelerator pedal beyond its normal point) to select a lower gear 'automatically'. This is particularly useful for getting up a hill or for quick acceleration when overtaking.

3 How to use the handbrake to make sure you don't move forward until you have pressed the accelerator pedal down far enough to overcome the weight of the car on the road.

### Creep

One danger in automatic cars is that sometimes they suffer from what is known as 'creep'. This means that the car can move forward slowly without pressing the accelerator pedal at all. If you know your car well, creep is not likely to be a problem; but when you are first learning to drive, creep can be potentially dangerous.

Automatics do make driving easier; they even make learning easier too. But you still need to learn all the rules of the road and the *differences* between automatic and geared cars in order to make the best use of an automatic.

You must learn all the correct techniques for driving an automatic car and, on the day of your driving test, you must show them to the examiner – right foot on the accelerator and right foot on the brake.

Remember that each 'automatic' car will have its own peculiarities listed in its handbook, and you will need to study these as much as you would for a manual-geared car.

# Pre-driving check, starting the engine, moving off and slowing down and stopping

## Pre-driving check

Every time you enter a car, you must check that it is safe before moving off. You do this by following a sequence of five steps.

The steps are easy to remember and you will soon find them a natural part of your everyday safe driving. The routine is known as

**DSSSM**

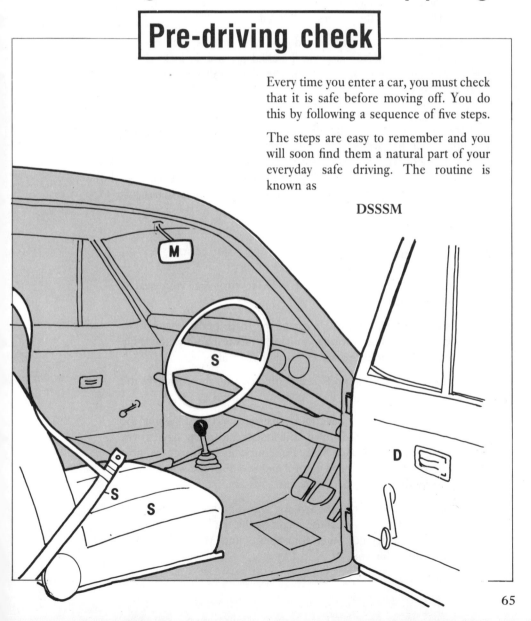

**D stands for Door**

Before you open the door, whether from inside or outside the car, make sure it is absolutely safe to do so without inconveniencing other road users.

Bear in mind that the same rule applies to the passenger door and to the driver's door if you are opening it on to the pavement.

When you are in the car, close the door straight away. Remember that car doors have a double-catch, so make sure it is not just held on the first catch only. Use your left hand to pull the door towards you and then push it away to ensure that it is properly closed; then, make certain *all* the other doors are closed.

It is not a good idea to lock *all* the doors. By all means, lock any rear doors if you have children and use the child-proof door locks if they are fitted. Check your car's handbook to see if and how the child-proof locks operate.

As the driver, you are responsible for ensuring that all the doors are properly closed before moving off. But on the day of your driving test, you don't have to carry this to the extreme of double checking the examiner's door. If you are not sure, you may ask him if his door is securely closed; but he will not be terribly impressed if you clamber around him to re-open and close the door that he himself has just closed.

**The first S stands for Seat**

Once you are in the car, you need to make sure that your seat is correctly adjusted.

- Check that you can press each of the three pedals right down to the floor without moving your body forward and, at the same time, you can hold the wheel lightly but firmly.

- Check that your bottom is firmly pressed into the corner of the seat and you can reach every control you need to use.

Remember that some cars have more than one way of adjusting the seat. Some have an up-and-down adjustment and many have a way to adjust the angle of the seat back. Find out which settings are most suited to your own comfort and control and re-adjust the seat to those positions *every* time you get into the car.

When you have driven for a few lessons, you will quite often find that the first seating position you chose might *not* be the best one for you. Don't be scared to try out other adjustments until you find the best particular position for you.

### The second S stands for Steering Wheel

When you have adjusted the seat correctly, you should find that you can now hold the steering wheel comfortably with your hands on the wheel at the ten-to-two or quarter-to-three position. If you find this position uncomfortable and feel more comfortable when your hands are lower than a quarter-to-three, the most likely cause is that your seat needs readjusting.

Once your seat is adjusted and your hands are comfortably placed on the wheel at ten-to-two or quarter-to-three, you need to check that you can move your arms around the steering wheel (as if you were turning a corner). You then need to make sure that there are no obstructions around you in the car and that nothing will prevent you from turning the wheel quickly and efficiently whenever you need to.

### The third S stands for Seatbelts

Most seatbelts these days are of the 'inertia' type. This means that the belts do not hold you back into the seat with any force *until* the car brakes suddenly. At that point, the belt locks in position and holds you firmly in your seat.

You should find that, once you are wearing a seatbelt, you hardly notice it is there.

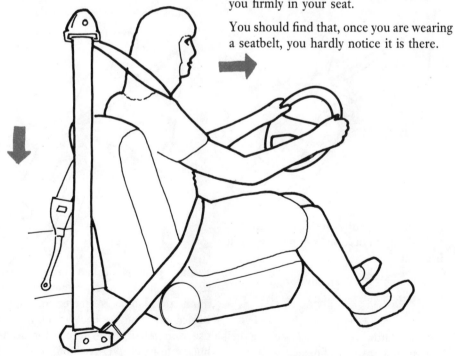

# Practice

Practise putting your seatbelt on.

- Lift the buckle with your left hand.

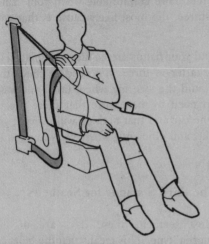

- Push your right arm through the loop.

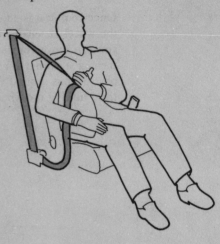

- Pull the buckle of the belt through to the locking device between the front seats.

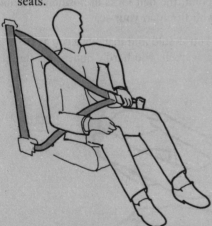

- Use your right hand to ensure the buckle is correctly fastened.

Because different cars have different methods of connection, you need to make sure that:

- the belt is correctly fitted around your chest and it is low over your hips

- you know how to release the belt whenever you've finished with it.

Practise putting the belt on and practise removing it. When you remove it, bear in mind that some seatbelts are spring-loaded and can fly back quickly. Again, use your left hand to return the seatbelt buckle to its correct position.

### The final M stands for Mirrors

Adjust the centre or window mirror so that you can get the best possible rear vision. Make sure that, when you adjust it, you keep your head and eyes in the normal driving position.

- Don't touch the glass with your fingers and thumbs – otherwise all you'll see are your fingerprints.

- Use your left hand placed behind the mirror to find the best position to frame the mirror against the back window.

One small point of warning. If the view behind seems very dark, remember that most mirrors have an anti-dazzle position operated by a small lever. Make sure you are not looking at the anti-dazzle image.

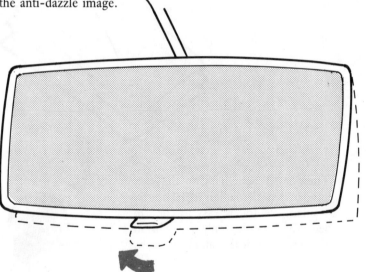

### DSSSM

You must check this sequence every time you get into the car. The first two or three times, you will probably need to be reminded to do one or two of the steps. But, very soon, you'll realise that you have learned this important car safety check and you will apply it automatically each time you get into your car to drive away.

# Starting the engine

Let's now move on to what to do when you switch on the engine. Again, there's another sequence to follow. It's shorter, but just as important:

**Handbrake – gear lever – starter**

Whenever you start or restart the engine of the car:

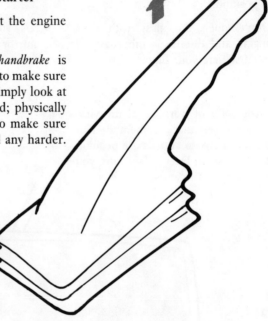

- First check that the *handbrake* is firmly applied. Pull it up to make sure that it is secure. Don't simply look at it and take it for granted; physically pull the handbrake up to make sure that it cannot be applied any harder.

- Then, move your hand to the gear lever and check that it is in the *neutral* position. Neutral is easy to confirm because it is the only position in which the gear lever can move freely.

● Finally, the key. Some older cars have two separate ignition switches: one is the key to switch on the ignition and the other is the switch or toggle to start the engine. Most cars, however, have only one switch.

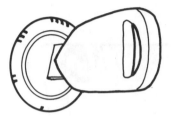

Turn the key and the moment the engine fires, release it immediately.

## Practice

Practise the sequence of handbrake, neutral gear and starter as often as you can. And don't forget that this sequence must be followed every time you start or restart the engine.

The sequence is perhaps most important if you stall the engine. The reason is that you may have stalled because you were in the wrong gear. Checking the handbrake prevents any danger of rolling back, and selecting neutral means that you are safe; then you can select first gear with certainty.

## Moving off on the level

Perhaps one of the most exciting moments in every learner-driver's life is when you actually move the car away from the rest – successfully on your own – under full control.

You can easily achieve this, even during your first lesson, provided you are well organised in advance.

Moving off follows a simple three-stage pattern.

**1** Always prepare the car to move off.

**2** Check all around you to make sure that nobody will be inconvenienced by your moving off.

**3** Only when you have decided that it is safe, move off.

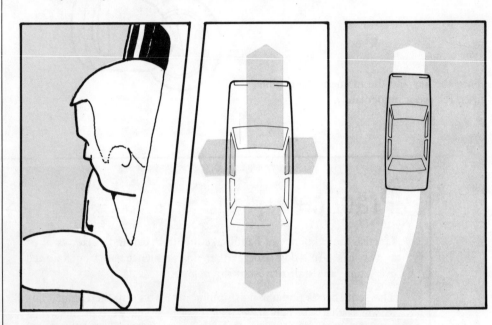

It can be broken down into these steps.

- Decide to move off.
- Look all round to confirm that you should be able to move off soon.
- Press the clutch down and select first gear.
- Press the accelerator pedal down slightly, hold it steadily there and listen for a constant humming noise from the engine. Your instructor will probably call this 'setting the gas'!
- Prepare the handbrake.
- Release the clutch pedal slowly until you hear or feel the car wanting to move against the handbrake.
- Keep both feet very still.
- Check the road ahead and the view behind you through your centre mirror and your door/wing mirrors.
- Look over your right shoulder.
- Decide if a signal is needed and, if so, whether to indicate 'right' or use a 'right' arm signal.
- If your view remains clear behind and safe all round – release the handbrake and move off by allowing the clutch to come up a little bit more, and, at the same time, gradually pressing the accelerator further down. Your instructor will probably call this last step 'giving a little more gas'.

**Using the choke**

The only time you change this sequence would be when the engine is 'cold'. In this case, you might find it necessary to use the **choke** – one of the minor controls used to compensate for the coldness by increasing the amount of petrol flowing into the engine.

Only use the choke when the car has not been used for some time.

As soon as you are driving the car and you find that you can control the amount of petrol flow by using the accelerator, push the choke control fully in.

# Changing gears

## Practice

Once you have moved off, you will then need to learn how and when to change gears.

The way to change gears is once more a set routine and one that you can practise in a stationary car with the engine switched off.

Only one word of warning about practising in the car without moving. There is a slight danger that you might be tempted to look at the controls as you use them.

The secret to all successful practice is to improve your skill and efficiency so that, when you are on the road, the actual movements will come easily to you.

**Changing up**

Here is the sequence for changing up through the gears:

- Check the traffic through your mirrors.

- Cover the clutch and put your left hand on the gear lever.

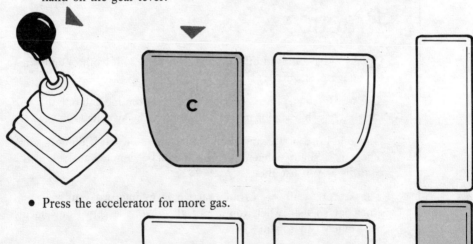

- Press the accelerator for more gas.

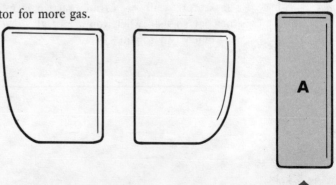

- Press the clutch down and take your foot off the accelerator at the same time.

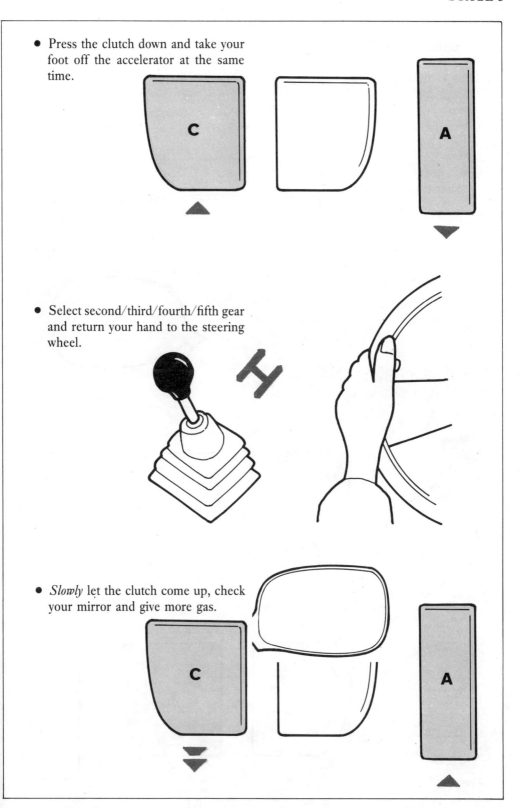

- Select second/third/fourth/fifth gear and return your hand to the steering wheel.

- *Slowly* let the clutch come up, check your mirror and give more gas.

### Changing down

Here is the sequence for changing down
through the gears.

- Check the traffic through your
  mirrors.

- Cover the clutch and put your left
  hand on the gear lever.

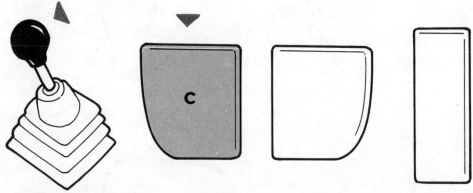

- Determine your correct speed and
  brake if necessary.

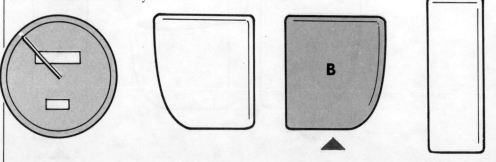

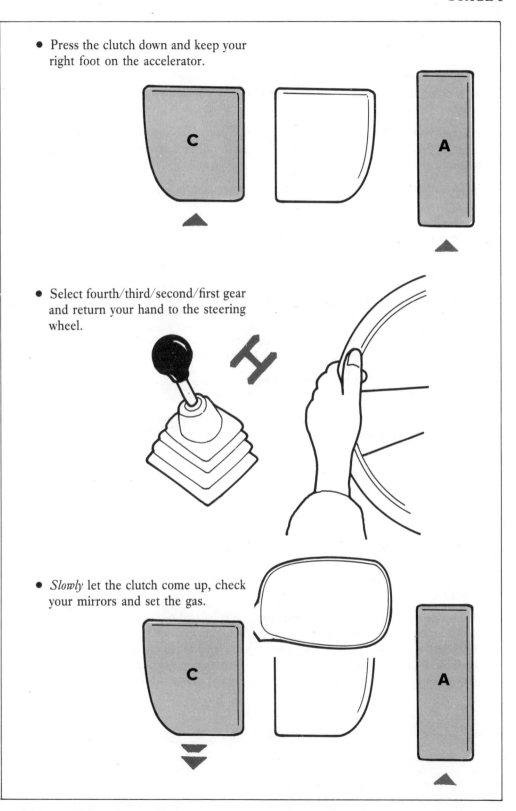

- Press the clutch down and keep your right foot on the accelerator.

- Select fourth/third/second/first gear and return your hand to the steering wheel.

- *Slowly* let the clutch come up, check your mirrors and set the gas.

77

### When to change gears

When to change gears is a more difficult question to answer. Although we touched on it in Stage 2, there are a few additional points to raise now.

People who have been correctly trained change gears 'subconsciously' – that is, they do so automatically. Such drivers would be hard-pressed to give you a rule about the correct moment to change gears.

In fact, most expert drivers change gears by listening to the noise of the engine. As the speed of the engine increases, the driver recognises the pitch at which he feels he should change up or down to a more effective gear than the one he is in.

Practise listening to your own car as you change up through the gears. You should be able to hear the difference in engine noise.

If you intend to build up to a high road speed, hang on to each gear for a little bit longer.

You also need to take into account how long it will actually take you to change gears and whether you are driving up or down a hill.

- If you are driving uphill, you must keep your foot on the accelerator all the time so you can maintain your speed.

- If you are travelling downhill, you can often take your foot off the accelerator and allow the engine to apply a braking effect on the wheels to control your road speed.

Take care *never* to think of 'coasting' – that is, selecting neutral, or driving with the clutch down, while you are driving along any road.

In Stage 2, you learned some guidelines for the correct speeds at which to change gears. Another guide is to use a 'rev counter' or a tachometer, if your car has one fitted. Your handbook will tell you the normal maximum speed you should use in any gear; if you change gear up at about half of this recommended engine speed, you will be about right.

If you don't have a rev counter fitted, you will soon find out that you can *hear* the correct normal engine speed to change up – once described to me as 'soprano', while the correct speed to change down was described as 'contralto'. Listen to your own engine again as you change up and then down through the four or five gears.

# Slowing down and stopping

Once the car is moving, it is very important for you to feel confident that you can stop the car easily. The simplest way is to remember that:

- Taking your foot off the accelerator will start to slow you down.

- Braking will then continue to slow you down.

- Braking progressively will allow you to adjust your speed to bring the car to rest at any particular point.

- Pressing the clutch down fully, just before you actually 'brake to stop', will avoid stalling.

It is not always necessary to change to a lower gear before you slow down and stop; it usually depends upon how quickly you need to bring the car to rest.

For example, if you are in fourth gear and intend to slow down before stopping, you should use third and possibly second and first gears to slow down and bring the car to rest gently.

But if you are in third gear and approaching a hazard, such as a set of traffic lights or a crossing, staying in third gear may well be a more sensible way to stop. Once more, it always depends upon the situation at the time.

The golden rule for you to follow at all times is: select the gear you will be *using* next *in advance*.

### The sequence for stopping is always the same

- Check your mirrors for any other road user who may need to be warned.

- Give a slowing down signal, usually by indicating left; the only time *not* to signal is when you *know* that no one would benefit from knowing that you intend to stop.

- Move your foot off the accelerator, cover the footbrake and then press the brake gently at first, but more and more as it is needed.

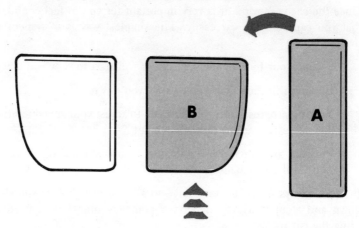

- Just before the car stops, press the clutch down all the way to the floor with your left foot.

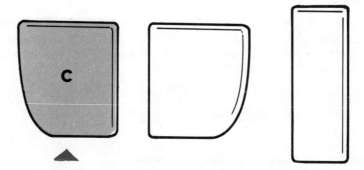

- Relax the braking effect with your right foot, so that the car gently comes to rest – rather than stopping with a jerk.

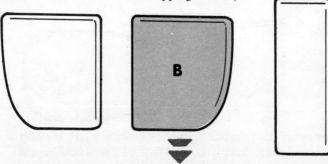

- As soon as you have brought the car to rest at your chosen spot, apply the handbrake, put the gear lever into neutral and relax both feet.

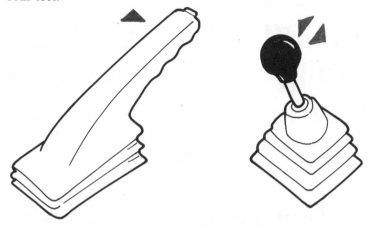

**Don't forget**

When stopping at the kerbside, you will be taking up a parking position. This means that you will need to stop closer to the kerb. You will, therefore, have to practise steering a line closer to the kerb than you normally do when following a safety line.

When you first begin to practise stopping, you will find that it is better to try to stop too soon and then ease off the brakes a little, than to leave it too late and need to brake suddenly.

Planned braking should always be smooth and unhurried; it is the hallmark of a good, skilled driver.

# Practice

In your first few lessons, it is well worth your while to spend a lot of time practising moving off, steering a little and then bringing the car to rest at particular points. This is a very important sequence to master.

Once you have it under your control, you will find that the confidence you have gained will enable you to move off and stop safely every time you want to.

# Moving off uphill and downhill, moving off at an angle and passing parked cars and other obstructions

## Moving off uphill

In Stage 3, you learned how to move off on the level. Now that you have mastered this skill, you will find that moving off on a hill is just as simple, with the addition of two extra items:

- More gas is needed if you are moving off uphill, and no gas if moving off downhill.

- Use the handbrake when moving off uphill and use the footbrake downhill.

Let's see how this works in practice.

First, moving off uphill.

To recap on the sequence for starting on the level: once you have decided to move off, you look around to make sure that you can do so soon. Then you press the clutch down and select first gear. You then set the gas and slowly let the clutch come up until you feel that the car wants to move against the handbrake. Keeping both feet still, you check the road ahead and behind, look over your right shoulder and indicate 'right' if necessary. If everything is still clear, you move off by allowing the clutch to come up a little bit more and pressing the accelerator down gradually.

Now, what you need to remember is that to give the car extra power to climb the hill, you need to give it more petrol or more gas (often your instructor will refer to petrol as gas). So, when you set the gas, you need to set it more than normal; and the only thing to remember about 'more gas' is – the steeper the hill, the more gas you need to use to climb it.

This is quite an important point and also very helpful.

When you've moved off before, on the level, you've always been a bit lucky about the decision to move away.

Now that you're moving off uphill, you will be in a better position to listen to the engine noise to tell you when the car is ready to move off.

- Set the gas a little bit more than usual, as you are already in first gear.

- *Slowly* let the clutch pedal come up until you hear the engine note change.

- At that point, keep your *feet* very *still.*

- Listen and you will hear the engine note change significantly.

What's happening is that the amount of gas needed to overcome the steepness of the hill shows itself in this drop of engine noise. The steeper the hill, the more noticeable the engine noise drop.

Try listening to the difference between the engine noise while starting off on the level and the noise when starting on a hill. The drop in engine noise is much more noticeable when moving off uphill.

This has a side effect which is very beneficial to you – that is, on a hill start, it enables you to recognise the precise point at which the car is poised and ready for a safe move-off. It is at this point that you release the handbrake.

# Clutch control

This is where you can show your 'skill' as a driver by demonstrating that the car will not move. The reason for this is known as **clutch control** – one of the most important skills for you to learn.

You should only use clutch control in first or reverse gears to manoeuvre the car – like, for example, on a hill start to enable you to move away at the precise moment you choose.

- If, when you remove the handbrake, the car starts to move forward, your clutch is too *high.* So, you must press the clutch down the slightest fraction.

- If, when you remove the handbrake, the car wants to roll backwards, your clutch is too *low.* So, you need to bring the clutch *slowly* up, the merest fraction.

# Practice

It sounds easy, but it needs a lot of practice.

And when you practice it, there's a trick of the trade to help you. It's made up of three steps.

1 What you are listening for is the change of engine noise, a drop from a louder noise to a softer one. So what you must do first is to *listen* for that change.

2 But this isn't always enough, so the second step is to look at the gear lever to see if it's trying to move sideways. Technically, this sideways movement is caused by the pressure from the engine trying to turn the gear lever around the transmission of the car. The car won't move, so the gear lever moves – or tries to move – instead.

3 The third step is to actually *feel* the vibration of the car as the engine desperately tries to move the car *against* the pressure of the handbrake. Because you are holding the handbrake in the prepared position, the car will not move; so you can feel the back wheels trying to move against the handbrake, the engine slowing right down and the vibrations as it wants to stall.

So, each time you practise an uphill start, remember the three-step trick of the trade.

- Practise *hearing* the engine noise drop.

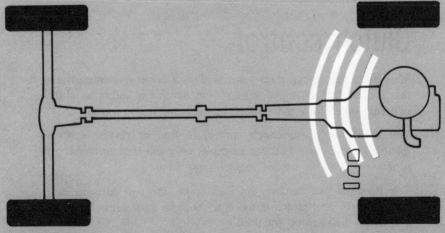

- Practise *looking* for the movement.

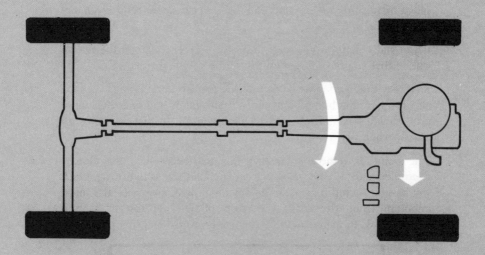

- Practise *feeling* the engine vibrate.

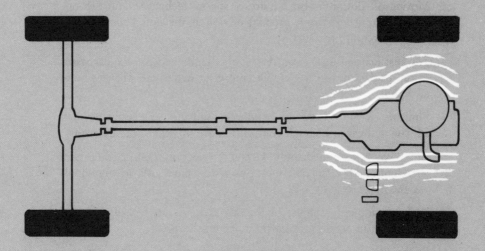

Once you have mastered this skill, you will soon come to realise that everything else you do when you learn to drive hinges upon it.

You will also soon discover exactly how little you need to vary the clutch from the position where the car wants to roll back, through the point where it is balanced, to the position where it wants to move forward.

# The biting point

Once you have found the point where the car is balanced – the so-called **biting point** – you will find that you can easily return to it and find it again and again.

If you stall, or try to move off in a rush and jerk the car, the reason will be that you have forgotten to use the clutch correctly.

So, every time you move off – both on the level and uphill – get the clutch up to this biting point, hold it absolutely still and then move off – slowly – completely under clutch control, so that *you* move off exactly when *you* want to.

The point to remember is that this particular skill, the clutch-controlled start, is your gateway to every skill there is in driving. Once you have mastered it, you can do anything, drive anywhere and, most important from a learner-driver's point of view, you can move on to learning how to manoeuvre the car using reverse and first gears.

## Moving off downhill

Moving off downhill also requires a special technique. But this one doesn't require the same amount of skill as the uphill start; it does however, require memory.

You just learned that if you release the handbrake and the car wants to roll back, you can use clutch control to determine when to move off uphill.

Similarly, if you release the handbrake and the car doesn't move at all, you still can use clutch control to move off when you are ready.

But, if you release the handbrake and the car rolls *forward*, you cannot use clutch control to determine when you move off; so you simply use the *footbrake*.

This is made even simpler by the fact that you don't need to set the gas when you prepare the car to move off downhill.

So the one sequence for moving off down-hill is simple.

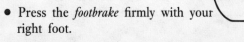
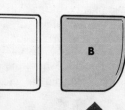

- Press the *footbrake* firmly with your right foot.

● Push the *clutch* down fully with your left foot.

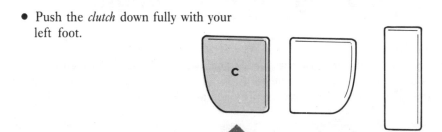

● Release the *handbrake* and keep the car stationary with your footbrake.

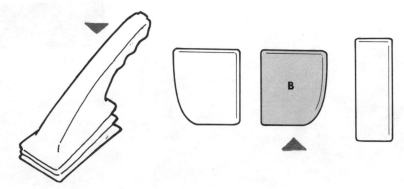

● Do a full observation check and, when you decide to move off, *slowly* let the clutch pedal come up to the biting point.

● Have another final look round and, if it is still safe to move off, take your right foot off the *brake*, set the *gas*, slowly let the clutch pedal come up fully, give more gas, check the mirrors – and you are away safely and smoothly.

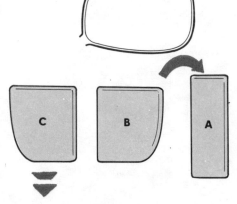

Every time you practise moving off, whether it's on the level, uphill or downhill, first of all check the gradient. If it is uphill or level, remember to use the clutch to control how and when you move. If it is downhill, remember to use the footbrake to help control the moving off.

# Moving off at an angle

When you first practise moving off, always try to do it from the side of the road, moving out from a parking position to a safety line. This is knows as **moving off** **at an angle,** and requires you to steer gradually to the right and then to the left to take up the safety line correctly, gently and as soon as possible.

When you have to stop and move off again in traffic queues or traffic lights, you will already be following a safety line. This is known as **moving off straight ahead.**

Sometimes you will find that you need to move away from the kerb at a much sharper angle when, for example, there is a parked car or other obstruction ahead of you. The secret of this is simple clutch control.

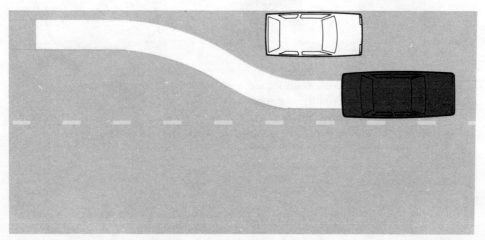

Clutch control enables you to move the car slowly forward, under full control, and gives you plenty of time to look and turn the wheel to the right and to the left – almost regardless of the amount of space you have available.

# Practice

At the beginning of your lessons, you should start practising moving off from behind a car or an obstruction about a car's length from you; you should be able to move off from here quite easily.

Then, gradually reduce the distance between you and the car ahead.

You will soon find that you need slow and steady clutch control in order to gain *more* time to turn the wheel.

Whenever you move away from the kerb – i.e., moving off at an angle – your aim must always be to follow a safety line as soon as possible.

And when you have an obstruction ahead of you, you have to be even more precise in how you act.

Remember the basic rule we discussed earlier about obstructions and the safety line:

You must try to keep at least a metre away from any obstruction while you are driving at normal speeds; if you drive any closer than that, you have to reduce your speed accordingly.

So if you allow about a half a metre clearance from the obstruction in front, you will find that under clutch control, you will be able to turn the wheel quickly to the right and then to the left, taking up your safety line as you go.

# Passing parked cars and other obstructions

The safety line is, of course, just as important when it comes to passing stationary and oncoming vehicles.

If you can make sure that you have about a metre clearance from any other vehicle, you can then make due allowance for any unexpected happening while you are driving past them.

Parked cars often fall into two categories.

1 Those cars parked in busy roads along the complete length of the road. Here, you need to drive slowly enough to keep an eye open for any potential danger like, for example, a man suddenly opening the door of his car.

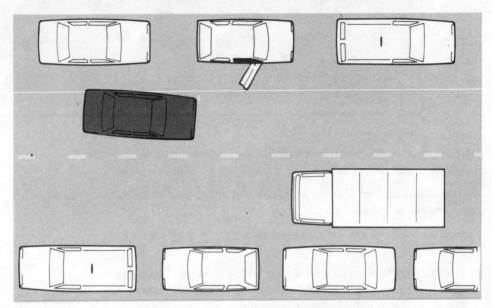

2 The other category is where you have an occasional car parked ahead of you in the distance that is restricting the width of the road. Here, you need to make a number of decisions:

- whether you go first or wait
- whether you signal or not
- whether you pull out early or late

All the answers depend entirely upon the circumstances at the time.

If you can move out, pass the vehicle and resume a safety line without inconveniencing any other road user, all your decisions are made for you.

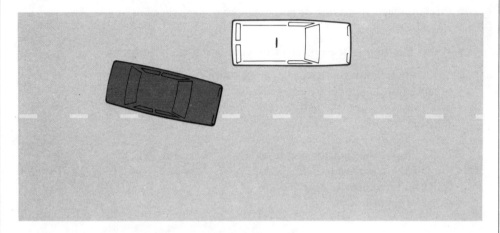

If, however, moving out means that any other road user is likely to be inconvenienced, you should not do it.

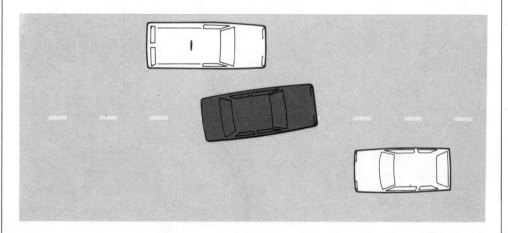

The sequence you should adopt must be as follows.

- See the problem up ahead.
- Check your mirrors to see what sort of traffic situation you have behind you.
- Check the traffic *well* ahead of you.

- Then, and only then, make a decision about your speed based on what you have seen.

- If necessary, give a suitable signal and then slow down or stop.

- If you have to slow down, decide if you need to brake or just to change to a lower gear. If a gear change is called for, remember to *increase the gas* slightly as you change down. This gives you the advantage of having *power* to increase your speed if you should need it.

- If it is safe to pass the car, maintain your speed and pass by.

- If you are following a safety line, a right-turn signal or indicator to move out should not be necessary. But if you do give a signal, take extra care to make certain that no one can read the wrong message from it.

- For example, the signal saying 'I am turning right into your road (path)' could lead another driver to pull out dangerously in front of you.

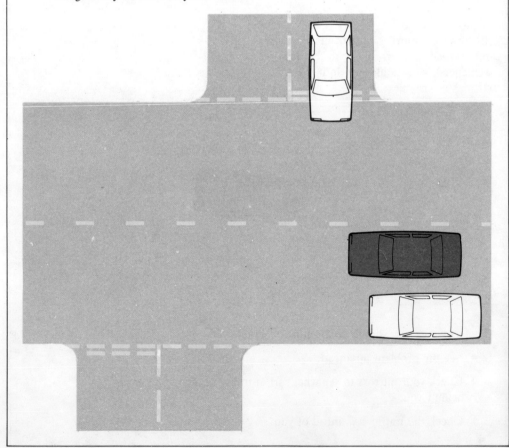

- If you decide to stop, do so far enough back so that you can see what is happening ahead of you.

- Never flash your lights to oncoming traffic either to invite them to move forward or to tell them to wait. The only signal they would benefit from is the slowing down arm signal.

Although priority is normally given to cars on the side of the road *without* the obstruction, you must always bear in mind that priority can only be given and never taken.

This is especially true when you have a heavy stream of traffic coming towards you or where traffic is coming up a hill at you. Drivers may be unwilling to slow down for you. So, do as your mother taught you: give way graciously.

# Practice

A useful exercise at this stage is to practise your hill starts and combine them with your signals for moving off.

Here is what you need to do.

- Prepare the car to move off.
- Still holding the handbrake, look all round.
- Release the handbrake and use your right arm to signal your intention to move off.
- *Then*, and only then, at the precise moment your right hand goes back on the wheel, allow the clutch to move the car slowly away from the kerb, taking up your safety line as you go.

The skill you are demonstrating in this exercise is that you are capable of moving the car at *exactly* the moment *you* choose.

Do this often and combine it with practice stopping the car in a parking position at different predetermined spots.

# Negotiating bends and junctions and turning left and right at corners

## Bends

You have already learned how to make a car move along a straight road. It now might seem a little bit peculiar to say that when you have to turn into bends and corners, all four wheels of the car follow different paths in relation to each other. Perhaps the easiest way to see this is to watch the tyre marks on a wet road when a car is turning a bend.

You can see that the front or steering wheels of the car revolve in a forward direction and, at the same time, turn the car to the left or right – to enable it to follow a new direction.

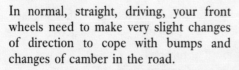

In normal, straight, driving, your front wheels need to make very slight changes of direction to cope with bumps and changes of camber in the road.

But on a bend, your change of direction is much more pronounced. The sharper the bend, the tighter your turn and, within reason, the slower your speed at the time you are taking the bend.

This illustration helps you to visualise the effect that brakes and steering have on your front wheels.

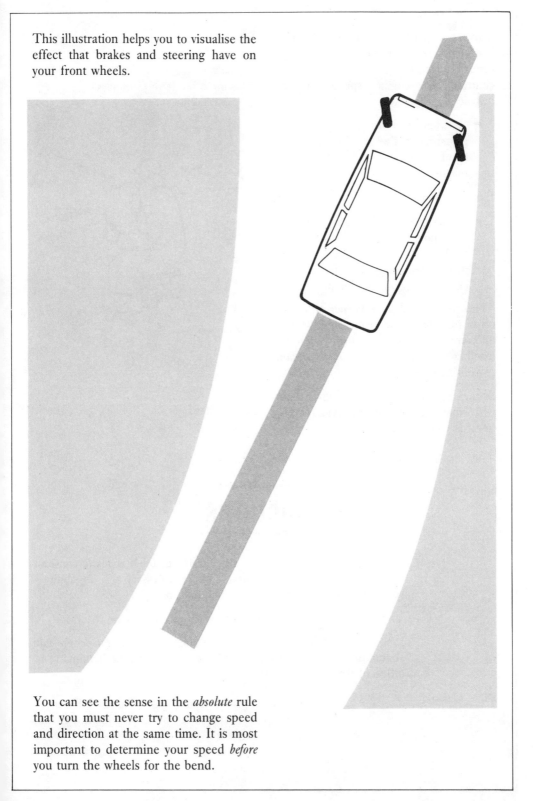

You can see the sense in the *absolute* rule that you must never try to change speed and direction at the same time. It is most important to determine your speed *before* you turn the wheels for the bend.

This is one of the reasons why most instructors prefer to use the term 'gas' instead of 'accelerator' for the pedal which controls the engine speed. If your instructor says to you:

- 'I want you to maintain steady pressure on the *gas* throughout the bend', you know precisely what he means.

But if he said:

- 'I want you to maintain steady acceleration throughout the bend', he might give you the wrong impression that he wanted you to *increase* your engine speed on the bend.

Think of a bend as a corner where no other road or traffic is involved; so your only concern when you turn a bend is whether you can stop safely *in the distance you can see to be safe*.

Always remember that you never know what may be parked, or even coming towards you, on a bend.

While driving in Ireland, I now always expect to go round a bend and find a little old lady sitting in the middle of my lane drinking a bottle of Guinness.

# Junctions

Where you have a corner with other traffic or other roads to consider and where a change of direction is either necessary or a possibility – you should regard that corner as a **junction**.

The key to coping with any junction is the way you approach it.

Junctions can take many forms. The one problem when people talk about them is that the talker and the listener are both thinking of different types of junctions.

This illustration shows the vast differences in shape, size, priority, complexity and, above all, in the amount of traffic using them and the number of options open to you.

At every junction, your basic sequence is always the same – MSM.

**Mirrors – Signal – Manoeuvre**

- As you approach a junction, look ahead, around and then behind using your **mirrors** to see what the conditions are and what options are available for you to choose from.

- Decide what **signal** to give to other road users so that they know what you intend to do.

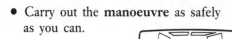

- Carry out the **manoeuvre** as safely as you can.

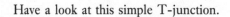

Have a look at this simple T-junction.

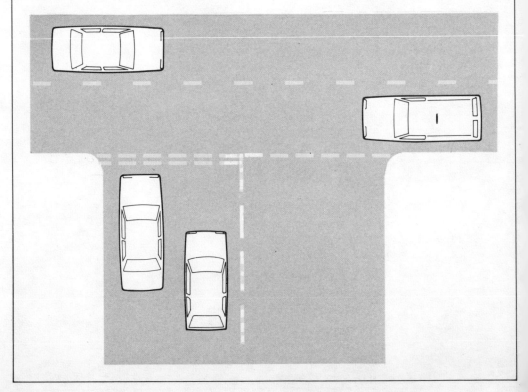

From the picture, you can see that a system of priorities normally exists which you will find easy to recognise.

- Those drivers travelling along the top of the T would normally expect to keep moving along without any interruption.

- But the driver with the leg of the T on his left would also be wise to look into the road on his left as he approaches the junction. If need be, he would also slow down to suit the possible danger.

- From the picture, you can also see a car travelling along the top of the T from right to left, intending to turn into the leg of the T. He would also expect to be able to complete his manoeuvre safely, as long as he bears in mind the golden rule of being able to stop safely in the distance he can see to be safe; he also has to be able to turn the wheels smoothly and correctly.

His priority is **number one**.

- The driver coming up the leg of the T intending to turn left into the top of the T would need to approach slowly and look mainly to the right, but also check to the left as well. Provided no one is approaching him from his right and the left is also clear, he can emerge safely and make his turn.

His priority is **number two**.

- The driver on the top of the T who intends to turn right into the leg of the T would need to slow down, observe the oncoming traffic and look into the road on the right, before making his turn.

His priority is **number three**.

- The final driver, the one travelling up the leg of the T intending to turn right into the top of the T, is the one who has to give way to just about everyone. This right turn is the most dangerous of all, as he needs to allow everyone else to complete their action before he can start his.

His priority is, therefore, **last**.

# Approaching junctions

Knowing how to approach junctions is probably the most important thing you will ever learn when driving a car.

Although clutch control is the greatest single *skill*, your *knowledge* of how to approach a junction correctly and your *attitude* towards the junction are the two most important factors in safe driving.

Your approach to any junction must always be the same: **Mirrors – Signal – Manoeuvre.**

- **Mirrors**
  After you have looked ahead at the road situation and your most likely course of action, you then need to check the traffic situation behind you. And don't forget to check for any traffic which may be sneaking up on either side (like cyclists or motor bikes).

  It is extremely important to check your mirrors and understand what is behind you and how other drivers may be affected by what you are about to do.

  Simply looking in your mirrors is, of course, not enough. You must *act* on what you see by telling other drivers about your intentions. This means that you need to make a decision regarding what signal to give.

- **Signals**
  The two most obvious signals are the right and left indicators. They are simple, easily seen and are also readily understood by traffic in front of you and behind you.

  The danger is when they are misunderstood.

  Therefore, the *timing* of your signal is very important, especially if you are turning into a particular road and you need to tell other road users which one.

  Even if you are approaching a crossroad and going straight on, a slowing down signal by arm is useful. But you should not need to give both a slowing down arm signal *and* a turning signal for the same purpose.

- **Manoeuvre**
  Assume that your manoeuvre is to turn left or right. The manoeuvre is broken down into another routine, **PSL:**

**POSITION** ⇨ **SPEED** ⇨ **LOOK**

## Position

Once you have signalled and only after you have signalled, you can take up a suitable position in the road to carry out the turn.

- If you're turning left, you will probably find that you will not need to change your position at all.

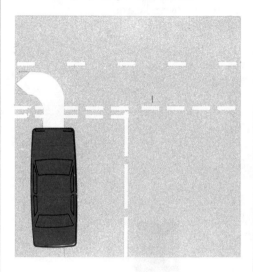

- If you're turning right, you may well have to move across to the right, nearer the centre line. That means taking a safety line from the right instead of the left.

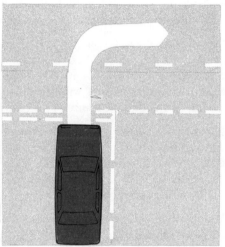

- If there are no white line markings on the road, you obviously need to be extra careful in finding a suitable position, particularly if you are turning right.

- If there are a number of lanes, then position yourself in the middle of the appropriate lane.

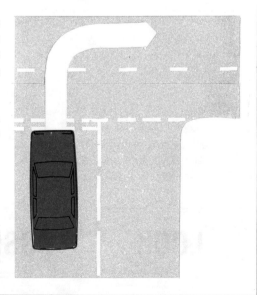

In any case, remember the extra dangers involved when turning right and the need for extra observation.

### Speed

The way you move out to the new position depends on the time and speed you have at your disposal – always do it gently, but always do it in good time. And this is the point at which you adjust your *speed*. This usually means you need to slow your speed down and select the most suitable gear for the turning.

You also need to keep a careful eye on your mirrors when you slow down, because other traffic may well now choose to overtake you. This is where your door or wing mirrors show their full value.

Although the way you slow down depends on the time and distance available, the most obvious and efficient way is to use your footbrake first and then select whichever gear is most suitable.

One clue to correct timing which often helps is to look at the hazard lines on your approach to a junction. When you approach a junction, you will often find *five* lines painted in the centre of the road.

If you have adjusted your speed correctly and selected the gear you think you will need at about the same time as you reach the *middle* of these five white lines, you will be in the correct position.

You are then able to start to **look** at the traffic situation on the right.

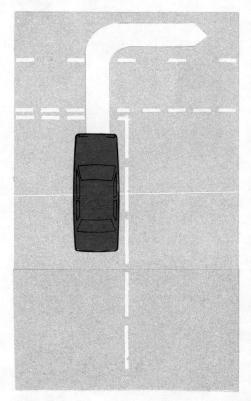

### Look

The looking part of the **PSL** routine can be broken down into three stages: **Look, Assess** and **Decide (LAD)**.

**LOOK ⇨ ASSESS ⇨ DECIDE**

- **Look**

  First of all you normally need to **look** *right* because the traffic approaching on your right will be nearest to your path.

- **Assess**

  Having looked to the right, then look *left* and **assess** the traffic situation. You now know if there is apparently nothing on your right, and probably nothing on your left.

- **Decide**

  A final look to the right will enable you to **decide** upon your action. The final decision is, of course, the most critical one for you to make.

Only make your decision when you are sure you have considered all the factors involved. If you're not absolutely sure, you need to slow down more, or, in some cases, stop. But if you do stop, try to stop in such a position that you are not in anyone else's way, and yet able to see clearly enough to make a decision to complete the manoeuvre when it is safe to do so.

**Here are the three sequences:**

**MSM**   Mirrors – Signal – Manoeuvre

**PSL**   Position – Speed – Look

**LAD**   Look – Assess – Decide

You should put these three sequences into operation every time you turn at a junction, regardless of whether your priority is number one, two, three or last.

You start the sequence as soon as you make the decision that you intend to turn or cross at a particular junction or crossroad.

## Practice

Because your timing on approach depends upon so many variables, the only way to learn how to cope is to practise as much as you can on every variety of road junction.

Start with the easy, straightforward junctions and then build up to more complex and busy ones.

In your early days of training, you will probably find that you will need to stop every time – whether the road is clear or not. This is just because your decisions require so much confirmation that stopping before you emerge is the only way you can convince yourself and your instructor that you can take in all the information.

You may well be able to keep moving on a simple left turn into a side road.

Eventually, you will find that you can also decide when it's safe to continue to move very slowly, usually in first gear, into a main road from a side road. Your ability to do this will depend on two factors.

1 As you learn to react better and quicker, you will be able to judge the speed and distance of oncoming traffic much better and quicker.

2 As you get more skilled at operating the car's controls, you will be able to keep your speed up to the rest of the traffic sooner.

**To summarise**

Follow this junction routine:

- Mirrors early enough to make initial decision.
- Signal clearly and unmistakeably.
- Position the car correctly.
- Adjust your speed by brakes and gears.
- Look all around before deciding to leave or join any road.

# Warning signs

County and borough council engineers are often very helpful in supplying and fitting warning signs on approaches to bends and junctions.

A cynical view might be that after three fatal accidents, they think it's cheaper to give you an advance warning of what's ahead. But if they haven't got round to it yet, try not to be the 'final fatality' that spurs them on.

The signs are put there for a purpose. The thinking driver will always read each sign as he sees it to find out what it means. For example, if an engineer bothers to put up a STOP sign instead of a GIVE WAY sign, you should try to find out *why* in the safest way possible.

On approaching a bend or junction, your aim must be to assess it thoroughly and every road sign will help you to carry out this assessment.

For example, assume you have arrived at the T-junction shown in this illustration:

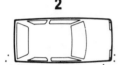

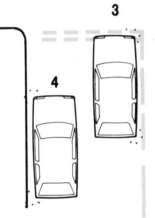

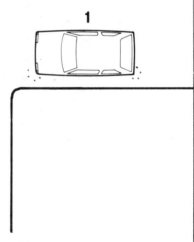

- Car 1 at the tip of the T is moving right to left and is turning left into the leg of the T.

- Car 2 at the top of the T is moving from left to right and is turning right into the leg of the T.

- Car 3 is travelling up the leg of the T and intends to turn right into the top of the T.

- Car 4 is also travelling up the leg of the T and intends to turn left into the top.

You need to make a total decision: to stop at the white line or to keep moving.

The simple answer must be – if there is any doubt at all about what you should do – *stop*. Stop where you can see and assess the oncoming traffic from all directions.

Only move off again when you are convinced that you can do so without inconveniencing any other road users, including pedestrians who may be crossing as well.

The secret of correctly emerging at a junction is based on your view of the road ahead. As you get closer to the junction which you are emerging into, your view of the road gets wider. But it is not until the last few feet that you have a clear view of the road and any hazards which might be lurking there.

There is a rule of thumb for judging how far forward you should be in order to make a decision to emerge: go far enough so you can see all that needs to be seen.

# Turning left

There are two types of left turn.

Each requires a slightly different approach, depending upon whether you are entering or leaving a side or minor road.

The initial approach in each case is the same:

**Mirrors – Signal – Manoeuvre.**

In this case the manoeuvre is:

**Position – Speed – Look**

This illustration shows a situation in which your car is turning left into a side road from a main road. Here's the procedure to follow.

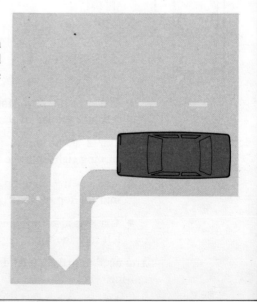

- Make sure your car is following a safety line.

- Look through your mirrors to see what traffic is around you, especially for traffic behind which will catch up to you when you slow down.

- Give the appropriate signal – the left-turn indicator is best.

- Start to slow the car down by decelerating and braking.

- Still following the safety line for the left turn, select the most appropriate gear for the turn (second is the most usual).

- As you arrive at the corner, you should be able to look into the road you are entering.

- Look into the road, make sure that you have no obstructions and then turn the wheel to the left.

- When the front wheels are facing the way you intend to go, return the wheel so that you can follow the safety line once more.

The critical moment is just before you start the turn. Not only must you look into the road you are turning into to assess and decide if it is safe, but you must also look into the mirrors once more – checking for any cyclists coming up on the inside and for any pedestrians who might wish to cross the road at that point.

So, the sequence to follow is:

**Mirrors – Signal – Position – Speed – Look – Assess – Decide**

This illustration shows a situation in which your car is turning left from the side road into the main road.

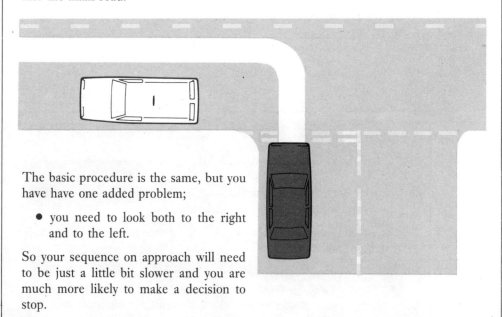

The basic procedure is the same, but you have have one added problem;

- you need to look both to the right and to the left.

So your sequence on approach will need to be just a little bit slower and you are much more likely to make a decision to stop.

In your early lessons, it is a good idea to stop at every junction when you emerge into a main road from a side or minor road. Carry on stopping at such junctions until your car-handling skills are good enough to allow you to make your own decisions safely.

When turning left from a side road into a main road, it is very important for you to remember your responsibilities to all other road users. Once more, the approach is just the same:

- mirrors followed by a signal (the left-turn indicator):

- maintain a safety line:

- adjust your speed and select the most appropriate gear (this time, first gear is most likely).

  A reasonable guide as to where and how far back this could be done is to look at the five hazard lines on approach.

- Make sure that you are at the speed you have selected and in first gear by the time that you have reached the *third* – or middle – of the hazard lines.

- At this point, you will find that you are now able to see more of the main road you are turning into than the road you are in.

- As you look to the right, your view of the main road, often called your *zone of vision*, should start to open up.

- Your *first* look to the right gives you a chance to see any immediate danger.

- Your *second* look to the left gives you a chance to assess any danger in that direction like, for example, the car parked too close to the corner in the illustration.

- Your *third* look, again to the right, gives you a bit more time to decide.

- If you are not sure about whether it is perfectly safe to emerge or if you need to look again to be positive, you should stop.

# Practice

In your early lessons, practise stopping at the white give-way lines and turn the wheel slightly to the left.

As you get more experienced, you will be able to decide for yourself the best place to stop.

With even more experience, you will be able to decide quite easily which roads do not require you to stop at all – provided, of course, you have had a good chance to look all around you on approach.

# Turning right

Turning right is easier than turning left.

The reason is that the angle you follow when turning the wheel to the right is less than the angle when you turn to the left – because your turn covers a longer stretch of road.

But, because of the extra traffic involved on a right turn, you are much more likely to have to stop.

This illustration shows a situation in which your car is turning right into a side road from a main road.

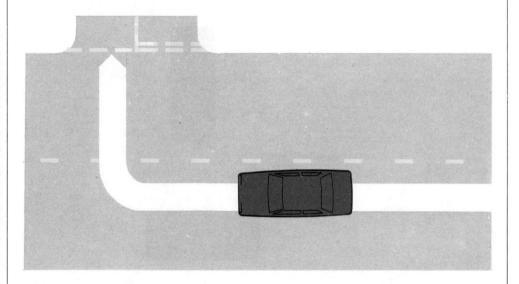

You follow exactly the same procedure as for turning left into a side road, with two added 'extras':

1 You should now follow the safety line to the right, shown in the illustration.

2 You will need to be prepared to stop at the safest possible point for *that* turn – at *that* time – in relation to the traffic situation.

Ideally, you want to position yourself in the mouth of the junction as shown in the illustration, so that you can turn to enter the road before any traffic leaves the side road and turns right into your main road.

But you will not always be able to control the situation. A lot will depend upon the flow of the other traffic as well as any parked vehicles which may be around at the time.

This illustration shows your car in a side road turning right into a main road.

Here, the position you take up is very important. It should be similar to that on the left turn, except for keeping a safety line on your right.

If you need to stop at the white lines, make sure that you can do so without interfering with any other traffic – whether they are turning or not.

What you must *not* do is aim for the white give-way line and stop there, regardless of who may be around.

Some larger vehicles, like the lorry in the picture, may have to use your road space to complete their own right turn.

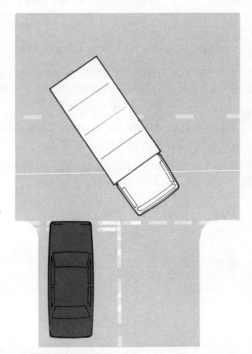

Positioning is most critical when you have to turn right from a narrow side road into a busy road, as in this illustration.

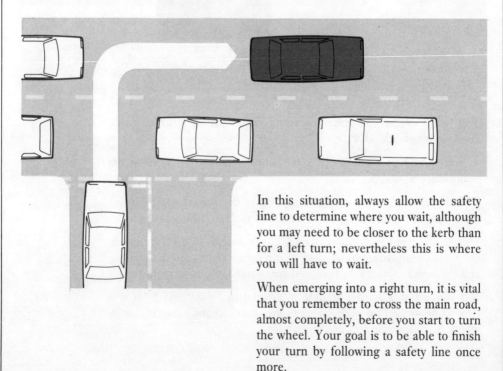

In this situation, always allow the safety line to determine where you wait, although you may need to be closer to the kerb than for a left turn; nevertheless this is where you will have to wait.

When emerging into a right turn, it is vital that you remember to cross the main road, almost completely, before you start to turn the wheel. Your goal is to be able to finish your turn by following a safety line once more.

# Right and left turns: a turning sequence

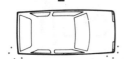

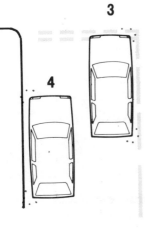

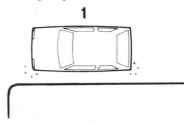

You will never have any problem with right and left turns if you can appreciate the need for a turning sequence.

The illustration shows a main road with a single side road off it on one side. Any traffic travelling along the main road can almost ignore the side road, provided full observation is given to any prospect of emerging traffic.

Those who are turning into or out of the side road fall into four categories, and each has a sequence to follow and a correct position in which to wait safely.

1 *Car 1* – turning left into the side road – should normally be able to make his turn without interference, provided there is no obstruction in the road he is turning into, and he gives way to any pedestrians who might be crossing.

2 Meanwhile, *Car 2* – turning out of the side road – will need to make sure that there is no traffic on his right, and that the road into which he is turning is also safe; therefore, he needs to look to the right, left and right again before deciding to stop or continue. If he stops, it should be where he can still see, but is safe.

3 *Car 3* – turning right into the opposite side road – would ideally like to wait at the intersection of the two white lines, but he is willing to be guided by traffic conditions. This position would enable him to complete his turn whenever a safe suitable opportunity presents itself.

4 *Car 4* is 'tail-end Charlie'. He must wait until everyone else has been able to go before he emerges into the main road.

So, the turning sequence is Car 1, then 2, 3, and 4.

# Turn-in-the-road, reversing and the emergency stop

## Turn in the road

When you are driving on your own, there will be many times when you need to go back where you came from. Although there are various ways to do this, the simplest and most obvious way is to continue on to a roundabout and come back (this assumes, of course, there's a roundabout nearby).

If there isn't one, you can also change directions by reversing round a right or left corner.

You should *not* change directions by a turn in the road, more commonly known as a three-point turn.

The **turn-in-the-road** is simply an exercise which has been devised by the Department of Transport for driving tests. It is included in the test so that you can demonstrate to an examiner that you can manoeuvre your car in a confined space like, for example, a car park.

Nevertheless, because it is part of the driving test training, you must learn how to turn your car effectively in the opposite direction – using first and reverse gears – and making the most efficient use of the space available.

## Practice

First of all, you need to find the most suitable space in which to practise the turn-in-the-road. Ideally, you should choose a road up to ten metres wide or about the width of three or four cars, as shown in this illustration.

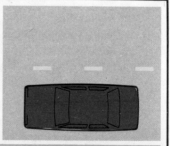

For your first few practice lessons, you can choose a road with a very gradual camber; for later lessons, you should select roads with all types of cambers.

This will prepare you for any type of road and camber you might meet on the day of your test.

When selecting a road, there are two things to avoid:

1 Roads which contain constant moving traffic.

2 Any road where children are playing.

This also applies to test routes, where examiners select roads for their test candidates.

When you find the suitable road, make sure you select the best place in that road for the manoeuvre – free from any obstructions like trees, lamp posts, or anything which might prove an extra hazard for you to cope with.

The objective of the turn-in-the-road manoeuvre is to turn the car round as if you were doing a U-turn. The three parts of the manoeuvre are shown in this illustration.

1 Driving forward and stopping near the kerb.

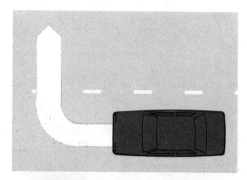

2 Reversing back across the road and stopping again.

3 Driving forward again.

Now for the detailed instructions for carrying out the manoeuvre successfully. Follow each step carefully and always refer to the accompanying illustrations.

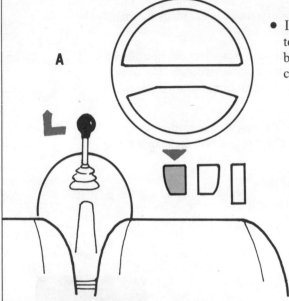

- In Illustration A, you prepare the car to move off by selecting first gear and by using clutch control to prevent the car from picking up speed.

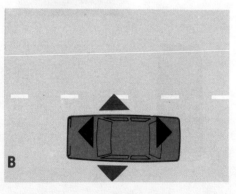

- In Illustration B, you make full observation checks to ensure that no one will be inconvenienced; if you are in doubt about the children walking on the other side of the road into your path, it is best to wait until they have passed.

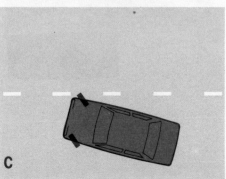

- Illustration C shows that you then slowly move forward and, at the same time, turn the steering wheel quickly and smoothly to the right.

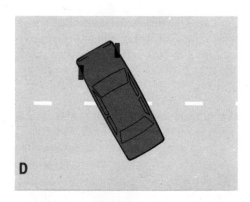

- In Illustration D, as the front of the car passes over the middle of the road, you should be on full lock and also prepared to press the clutch down again gently to slow the car down just a little bit.

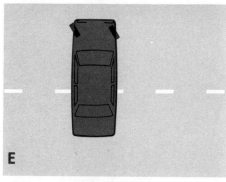

- Illustration E shows that when you are about one metre from the kerb, you cover the brake and, at the same time, turn the steering wheel fully to the left.

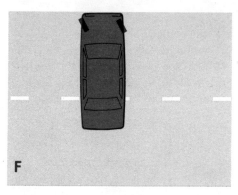

- In Illustration F, you gently brake without allowing any part of the car to overhang the kerb.

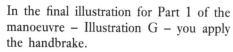

In the final illustration for Part 1 of the manoeuvre – Illustration G – you apply the handbrake.

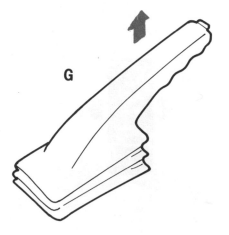

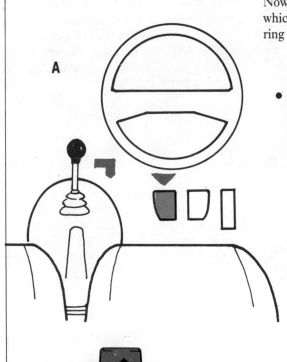

Now look at this next set of illustrations, which show the steps to follow in manoeuvring the car back across the road.

- Illustration A is the first step and is the same as Part 1 in that you again select your gear – in this case reverse gear – and get the car under clutch control.

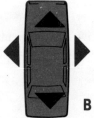

- Illustration B is to make full observation checks once more, but this time you need to look to the left first (because of any oncoming traffic), and then to the right and left again.

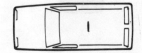

If there is any traffic coming from the right, as there is in the illustration, you should *wait*.

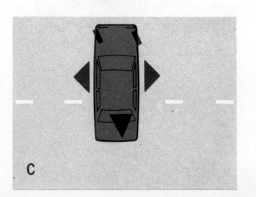

- If there is any traffic from the left you should let them decide whether you should wait or not; when it is clear, as shown in Illustration C, move backwards, *under clutch control*, carrying out both rear and side observation checks.

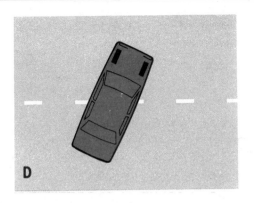

D

● Illustration D shows that once the car is over the middle of the road, you need to use the clutch very carefully to keep your speed down. This will also give you time to start to turn the wheel back to the right, on full lock.

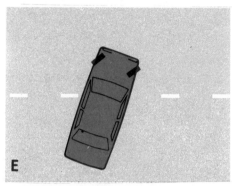

E

● Illustration E shows that, just before you reach the kerb, you cover the brake and turn the wheel sharply to the right.

F

● In Illustration F, you gently brake to stop fairly close to the kerb, but not overhanging it at all.

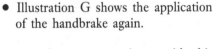

● Illustration G shows the application of the handbrake again.

As you gain more experience with this second part of the manoeuvre, you will be able to demonstrate your skill by only going back far enough to give yourself enough room to complete it safely.

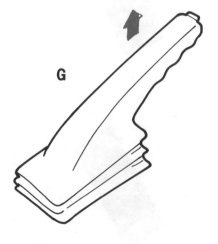

G

Moving off for the third leg is the easiest manoeuvre of all.

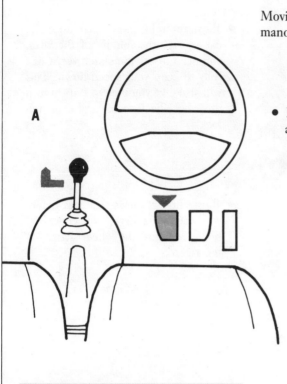

- In Illustration A, you select first gear and get clutch control once more.

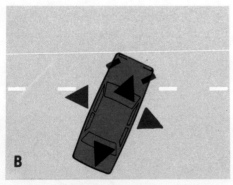

- Illustration B shows you making full observation checks, taking care especially to look over your *left* shoulder for blind spots.

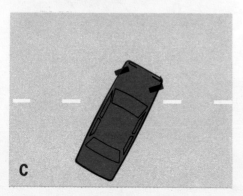

- When you are convinced it is safe to do so, as shown in Illustration C, move slowly forward, turning the wheel to the right, but keeping your eyes open for any traffic all the time.

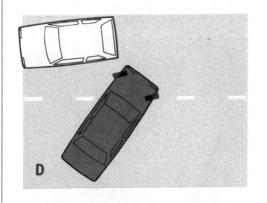

- If you are not obstructing the passage of any oncoming traffic from your left – as shown in Illustration D – it is usually best to allow them to keep going, if they will.

- However, if you are obstructing traffic from your left, as shown in Illustration E, it is best for you to get out of their way, if you are allowed to do so. But the rule must always be to allow other traffic to take the decision to wait or move.

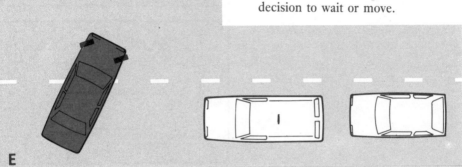

One final point about the third leg: make sure you only turn the wheel far enough to get across the road. You do not need to stay on full lock too long, or you won't be able to get back to the normal keep-left position.

Here are five extra things to remember when you're practising the turn in the road.

- Choose a safe road and the safest place in that road.

- Make sure your observations cover every possible contingency.

- Remember that *you* are the driver doing the unusual manoeuvre.

- Keep the car moving slowly by the efficient use of clutch control.

- Practise steering by turning the wheel quickly in each direction.

The three essential points for you to remember every time you think of the turn in the road:

**1** Good clutch control → **feet**

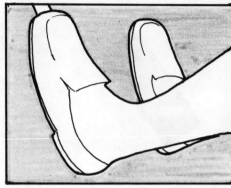

**2** Efficient steering → **hands**

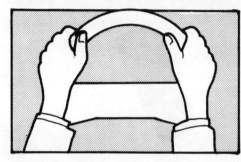

**3** Total observation → **eyes**

In other words, during each of the three legs, you need to:

- get clutch control;
- look all around *before* you start to move;
- work out which way to turn the wheel;
- continue your observations as you move, with your final observation always being to look towards the place where you intend to stop.

Remember that each decision you make needs to be a conscious one based on clutch control, efficient steering and total observation.

# Reversing

Whenever you need to reverse, the golden rule to remember is that all other road users expect you to be moving forwards – therefore, it is your total responsibility to ensure *their* and *your* safety.

Never reverse more than is necessary to carry out the manoeuvre safely. Reversing for more than a 'reasonable' distance can be potentially dangerous.

Remember that when you select reverse gear, you do not change any of your other car controls. The same wheels steer (except they are now at the back of the car), and have the same effect on the car. But do bear in mind that it takes longer for your steering in reverse to take effect.

# Reversing in a straight line

Reversing in a straight line is easy, provided you follow these five basic rules:

**Five rules for reversing in a straight line**

1 Control the car by clutch control and avoid picking up speed.

2 Make sure that you can see it is safe to reverse.

3 Take full observation checks – including all blind spots – before you start to move.

4 Look at where you want to go and, if necessary, adjust your seating position to ensure that you can see clearly through the back window.

5 Only move when you are sure it is safe to do so.

If you want to steer the car to the right or left, you also need to look in front of you before you do so to make certain that you are not likely to inconvenience any other road user when you change your direction.

# Reversing to the left

This is the most common type of reverse you are likely to use and is quite straightforward.

This set of illustrations shows the steps to follow to carry out successfully the reverse to the left.

- Illustration A shows your car driving up to the road into which you intend to reverse, stopping before you pass it and looking into the road to ensure that it is safe to reverse.

**A**

- In Illustration B, you drive past the road and stop in a position where you can *just* see the kerb on your side in your rear window.

**B**

- Illustration C shows you looking all round to make sure that you are not likely to inconvenience any other road user when you move off.

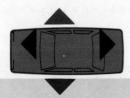

**C**

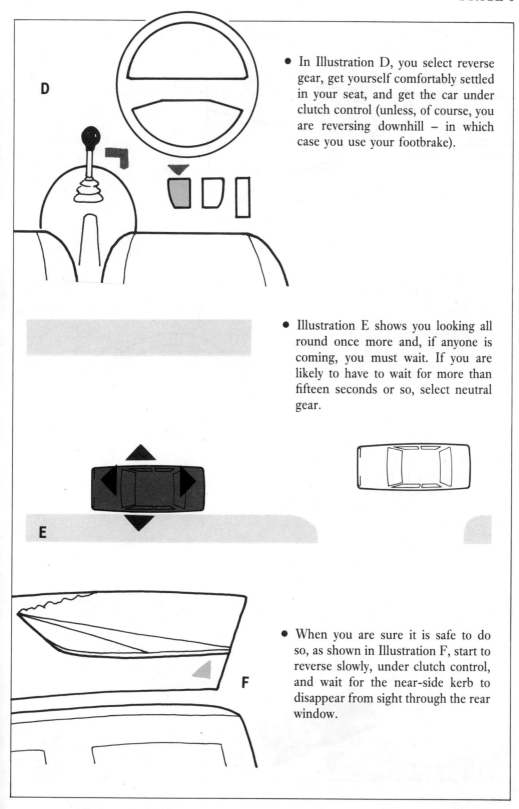

- In Illustration D, you select reverse gear, get yourself comfortably settled in your seat, and get the car under clutch control (unless, of course, you are reversing downhill – in which case you use your footbrake).

- Illustration E shows you looking all round once more and, if anyone is coming, you must wait. If you are likely to have to wait for more than fifteen seconds or so, select neutral gear.

- When you are sure it is safe to do so, as shown in Illustration F, start to reverse slowly, under clutch control, and wait for the near-side kerb to disappear from sight through the rear window.

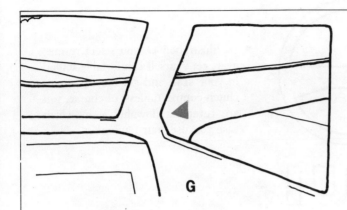

G

- In Illustration G, when the kerb reappears again in the side window, you must look all round to the front just to make sure it is safe to start the turn.

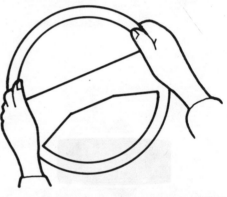

- In Illustration H, you start to turn the wheel to the left by pulling the wheel down with your left hand. The steeper the angle, the quicker your turn; the gentler the angle, the slower you turn the wheel.

- When you can see into the road you are entering, as shown in Illustration I, look out for any oncoming road users (including bicycles) and be prepared to stop and move forward again if necessary.

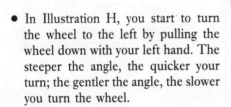

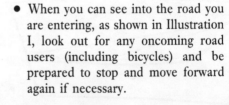

I

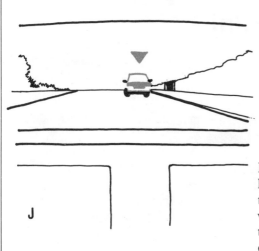

J

- When you can see that the road you are entering is clear, as shown in Illustration J, look out of the back window until the road appears straight and then straighten out the car by turning the wheel sharply to the right. A useful hint here is to fix your eye on a distant 'target' to use as an aiming mark for reversing.

Do not look at the pavement nor at the lamp posts nor at anything else fixed on the pavement. The ideal target is the windscreen of a car positioned some twenty or so metres behind you, if one exists.

- When your car is parallel and near to the kerb, as shown in Illustration K, continue to reverse in a straight line, keeping as close to the kerb as possible.

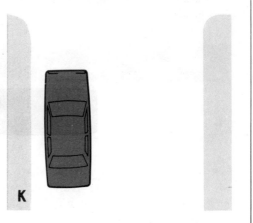

K

- In Illustration L, you bring the car to a stop – using the clutch, gently braking, putting the handbrake on and putting the gear level into neutral.

L

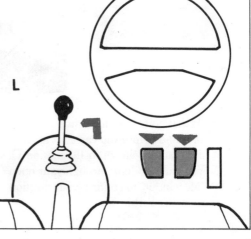

# Reversing to the right

Reversing to the right is similar to reversing to the left, but there are one or two important differences.

**A**

- First of all, you need to start by going on to the wrong side of the road, facing any oncoming traffic, as shown in Illustration A.

**B**

- Then you need to reverse slowly, looking through the rear window until you are in a position to look all round before you enter the new road on the right, as shown in Illustration B.

**C**

- At that point, you must stop and look all round before you can start to enter the road, as shown in Illustration C. You can also look through your open side window to confirm your position from the kerb.

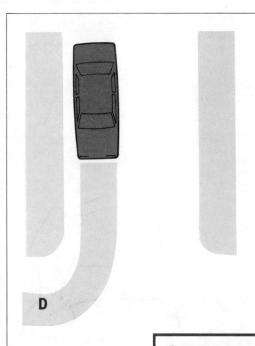

D

- Once you are around the corner, as with the reverse-to-the-left, you look through the back window to continue reversing as close to the kerb as possible, as shown in Illustration D.

You must stop at both of these points because you will need physically to change your seating and looking position.

With all reversing, remember you are doing the unusual thing. And if there is any possibility of causing a nuisance, you should move out of the way.

# Stopping in an emergency

The emergency stop is often thought of as a test manoeuvre because, on the driving test, the examiner asks you to stop 'as in an emergency'. His reason for doing so is to enable him to assess what sort of reaction you will give when such an occasion does arise during your normal driving.

Instruction about how to cope with emergencies should be given at a very early stage in your driving lessons.

You should begin by looking at the back page of *The Highway Code*, which gives the minimum stopping distances. Not only must you learn these by heart, you must also understand what they mean.

During your driving lessons and practice, you should be able to apply these distances to whatever traffic is ahead.

Even so, there will be occasions when the distances are drastically reduced, as in foggy weather or where a child or other person runs in front of you and you have to stop as quickly as possible, bearing in mind that you cannot stop dead.

When you do stop in an emergency, you must prepare yourself to apply all your efforts to stop the car within the safest distance you have in front of you.

## Four rules for stopping

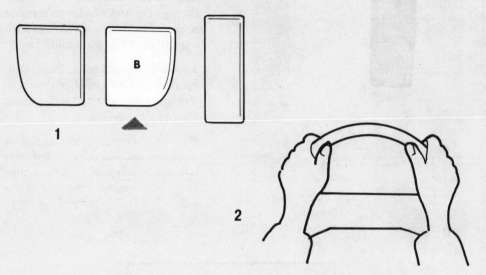

1 Make the most of the time available by braking as early as possible.

2 Make sure you have firm control of the steering at all times by keeping both hands on the steering wheel.

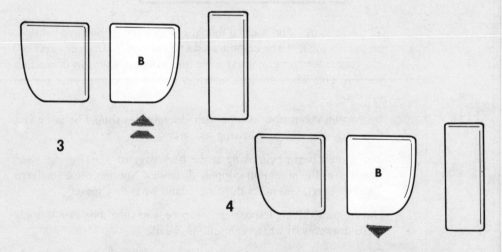

3 Brake firmly – progressively – and increase the pressure until you feel the road wheels wanting to lock (that is, stop revolving).

4 *Before* they lock, release the brake pedal enough to allow the wheels to continue revolving – thereby avoiding any danger of skidding.

Skidding occurs whenever the car is travelling faster than the wheels allow.

If the momentum of the car is so great that it overcomes the grip of the tyres on the road surface, you may skid.

You can avoid this by sensing the movement of the car. Once you have released the brakes lightly and the wheels are revolving again, you must apply progressive pressure on the brakes once more. This is called 'cadence braking' and it will give you complete control of the car and allow you to stop as quickly as possible for that speed, on that road surface and in those conditions.

# Practice

- You will need to practise stopping quickly.

- In your early lessons, practise stopping quickly while you are moving at speeds below ten or even five miles per hour.

- Once you have mastered this, gradually increase your speed until you are able to stop quickly, but safely, at any speed – and on most road surfaces.

- There is no need to use the mirrors before you start to brake; but you should glance in them as you commence braking.

- Make sure that your instructor is confident that no other road user is around you and that no one is behind you when he asks you to stop suddenly. He must be in complete control of the situation.

### One golden rule

When you stop in a genuine emergency, remember that what you look at is what you aim for – therefore, always look where you want to go and never at what you are trying to miss.

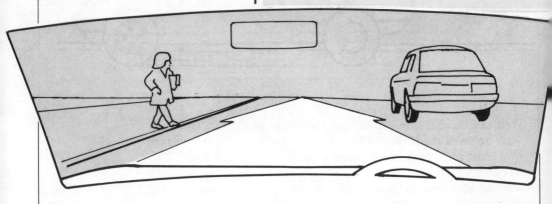

Here is the sequence to follow when an emergency arises.

- Take your foot off the accelerator and on to the footbrake;

- Brake firmly and progressively with the intention of stopping as quickly and safely as possible.

- If the wheels start to slide at all, release the pressure on the brake and then apply it once more until you slow down completely and stop.

- Apply the handbrake.

- Select neutral gear and then relax your feet.

Notice that the clutch pedal has not been mentioned at all. That's because the clutch is never used when you have to stop in an emergency.

Just before the car actually stops, you can press down the clutch to avoid stalling. But stalling does not affect stopping at all.

If you should stall, remember that the engine has been helping you to slow the car down. If you were to press the clutch pedal down too soon, you would then be allowing the car to run free.

# Crossroads and junctions, road markings, one-way streets and roundabouts

## Crossroads and junctions

The basic difference between a crossroad and a junction is that at every junction you have to decide whether to enter or emerge – to either turn right or to turn left. At a crossroad, you need to make the same decisions, plus one more – it is also possible to continue straight ahead. All too often drivers tend to ignore the crossroad altogether, which can create a potentially dangerous situation. Therefore, you need to weigh up every crossroad carefully and make a decision about what action to take based on all the information around you.

**Right of way versus priority**

Before going any further, it's necessary to clear up a common misunderstanding about the phrase, 'right of way'. It's not so much the phrase itself which is wrong, but the fact that so many people use it to mean different things. So instead of the phrase 'right of way', substitute the word that the Department of Transport uses – 'priority'.

As you approach some crossroads, you will see immediately that you have priority.

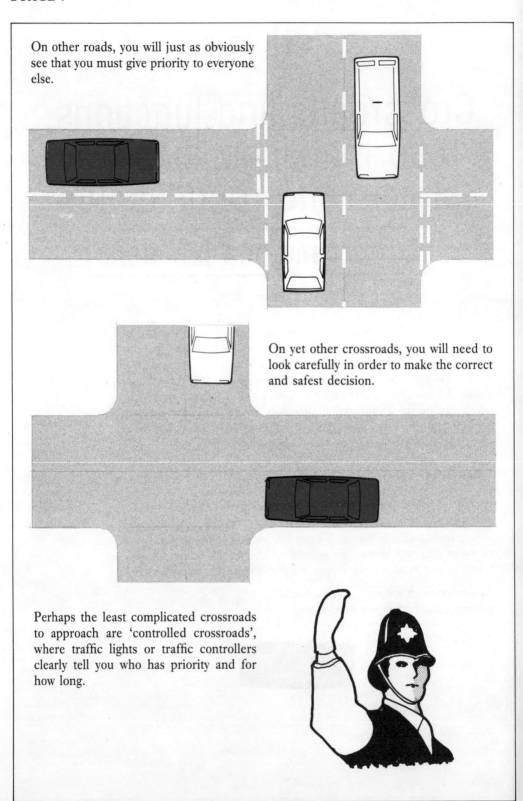

On other roads, you will just as obviously see that you must give priority to everyone else.

On yet other crossroads, you will need to look carefully in order to make the correct and safest decision.

Perhaps the least complicated crossroads to approach are 'controlled crossroads', where traffic lights or traffic controllers clearly tell you who has priority and for how long.

# Mirrors – Signal – Manoeuvre

On all crossroads you must approach them safely enough to enable you to follow the **MSM** sequence of **Mirrors – Signal – Manoeuvre**. It is not enough simply for you to look right, left and right again as you approach the crossroad. Instead, you need to assess the whole situation thoroughly – and that means continuing to look in all directions to locate any dangers which may exist or arise when you arrive at the critical point of having to make a decision. The phrase you should use is taking 'full observations'.

If you are on a good wide road, as in this illustration, with clear visibility on approaching the crossroad (two small side roads opposite each other), there may be no need for you to slow down at all. It is clear that you have priority and that the approaching traffic is giving priority to you.

But if there is any doubt about your priority, or about whether you can rely upon other traffic giving priority to you, you must slow down and make sure that you can stop safely.

If you have priority, you must still carry out full observations of the situation around you.

If you have to give priority to other traffic, you must follow exactly the same three sets of sequences you do for approaching junctions.

- MSM, Mirrors – Signal – Manoeuvre

- PSL, Position – Speed – Look

- LAD, Look – Assess – Decide

On some occasions, you will come across crossroads with no apparent or obvious priority, like the one in this illustration. Here you must be prepared to allow everyone else to take priority over you.

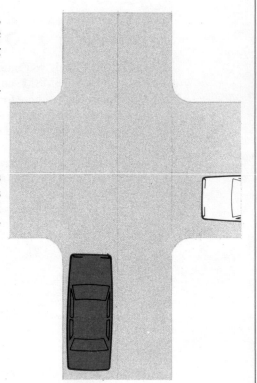

Or, as in this illustration, if your visibility is obscured by hedges, parked cars or any other obstructions, you must be fully prepared to stop – preferably in a place where you *can* see – and then only move on when you have checked completely that it is safe to do so.

If you are using crossroads like the two you have just seen on your lessons, you should go across these sorts of roads in *both* directions, so that you can get a better idea of what other road users might be thinking and doing.

Similar problems might arise on some crossroads where signs and white lines are clearly painted across the roads, but rain or glaring sunshine tends to obscure them.

Once more, it is worthwhile looking at the approach to a crossroad from both sides to see what is obscured and what sort of errors other road users might make. This situation is often made worse by the fact that white lines are not always painted in the same direction as the road surface is built, as shown in this illustration.

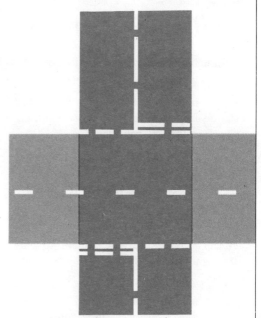

# Road markings

Road markings themselves tell you a lot about the roads you are using. A golden rule must be, if someone has bothered to paint something, it is worth your while bothering to find out why and what it could mean.

Road markings can be categorised into three groups:

- information lines
- warning lines
- compulsory lines

# Information lines

Information lines are usually in the form of direction arrows or lane markings.

When you are following a safety line, you will usually find that you are centrally placed in the left-hand lane.

If you decide to overtake and pass other traffic, you will occasionally have to change lanes. To do so, use the **MSM** (**Mirrors – Signal – Manoeuvre**) routine.

When you do need to change from lane to lane, make sure that you do so only after you are absolutely certain it is safe to do so.

Direction arrows in the road like those in this illustration will guide you to take specific lanes from time to time. Keep your eyes open, always looking for guidance from the arrows – especially when you are driving in busy town traffic.

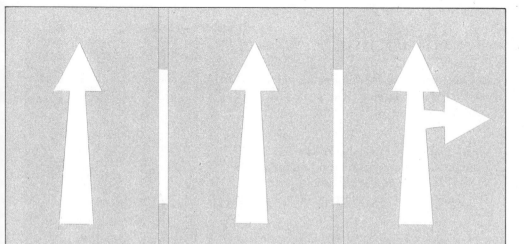

You will often find 'change' of arrows immediately after a left or right turn. For example, this illustration shows you turning right and ahead of you there are arrows allowing you to go straight on or turn right. Because you are in the right-hand lane, look ahead for traffic which may be turning right, particularly if you intend to go straight on. This especially applies where arrows direct you to continue ahead or to turn right in this lane.

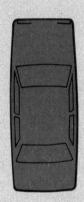

The problem does not occur quite so often with arrows allowing you to turn left or go straight ahead, because traffic turning left is not as likely to be held up as traffic turning right.

The golden rule with regard to driving in lanes is that if you are driving in traffic and find yourself in the wrong lane, it is usually better to go the wrong way – and find your way back – instead of trying to change lanes without taking the necessary MSM precautions. At the same time, always keep a lookout for other drivers who may be in the wrong lane themselves and intend to change lanes without warning or without using their mirrors effectively.

# Warning lines

Warning lines, like the information lines, are there for a purpose. The centre line between opposite lanes of traffic is the most common one.

One useful rule to remember is – the more paint on the road, the more care you need to take. Hazard lines are a case in point, and double white lines illustrate the paint rule.

- If you see double white lines with the solid line nearest to you, as in Illustration A, then you must not cross them at all.

- If, however, you see broken lines nearest to you, as in Illustration B, then you can cross, provided you are certain that it is totally safe to do so.

- Sometimes you will find that the centre double white line is widened out to form a 'hatch marking' as in Illustration C; it is there to emphasise the danger of a situation (in this case a keep-left sign) and to ensure that lines of traffic coming in the opposite direction will keep well clear of each other.

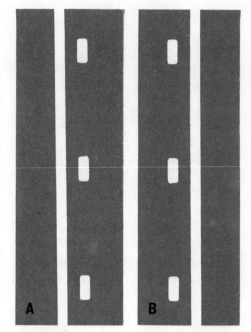

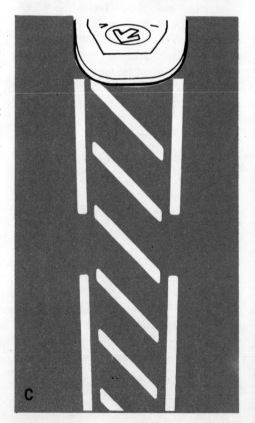

# Compulsory lines (hatch markings)

Compulsory lines fall under two headings, depending on whether the *outer* lines are solid or broken.

- If they are solid, you must treat them exactly the same as if they were part of a double white line system.

- But if the outer lines are broken, you can cross them provided it is safe to do so.

You will often find that large lorries need to cross over compulsory lines to turn safely. And never believe that other traffic will not cross them as well.

Stop and Give Way lines at the junctions of minor roads with main roads are two other examples of compulsory lines.

Always remember that the Stop lines mean that you must come to rest and apply the handbrake, no matter how briefly – and then move off when it is safe. It may also be necessary to stop at a Stop line and then move forward to a new position where you can see, stop again and wait until it is safe to move forward once more.

Give Way lines, on the other hand, mean that you do not need to come to rest provided you allow any other road user to take priority over you.

Generally speaking, the normal sign used at the junction of minor roads with major roads would be a Give Way sign. It enables you to use your own initiative and observation to decide whether to stop or not. If, however, the Department of Transport decides to use a Stop line instead, there must be a good reason for their decision – and therefore you need to stop to see what that reason is.

At crossroads where there are no lines at all, give precedence to traffic travelling in any direction and be prepared to give way or stop regardless of which way you are going.

And on roads where you appear to have priority because the Give Way or Stop lines are in your favour, you still need to look, just to make sure that the road user coming up to them is prepared to obey the road markings and signs and actually to give way. Sometimes white lines cannot be seen and occasionally some drivers who do see them ignore them anyway.

# One-way streets

To most people, one-way streets seem to be so obvious that they take them for granted. But there are one or two important rules to remember about them which will make driving on one-way streets even safer than on normal two-way roads.

When you enter a one-way street from a side road, your main concern will be from the right only if you are turning left, and from the left only if you are turning right.

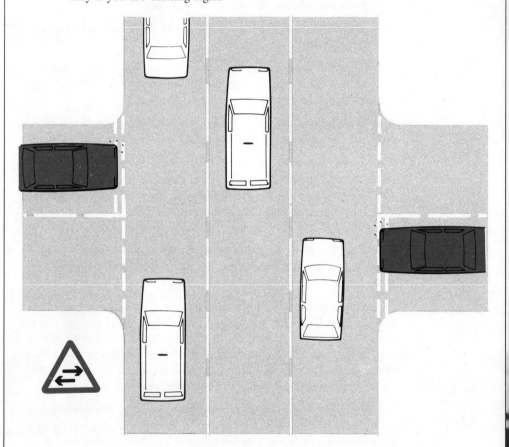

Of course, you still need to look the other way as well for non-conformists travelling up the one-way street the wrong way and for obstructions like, for example, a large parked lorry.

One of the advantages of one-way streets is that you can take up your right-turn position very early, sometimes as soon as you join the one-way street.

Another advantage is that the traffic often flows in the same direction in two, three or more lanes.

You should always travel in the most suitable lane and stay in that lane; avoid changing lanes simply as a means of overtaking or making better progress.

At the same time, always keep an extra eye open for people overtaking you on both sides.

In three-lane one-way streets, you may prefer to use the centre lane for travelling straight ahead; this avoids parked cars and left-turning traffic. But always be guided by lane directions and signs.

When turning right from one-way streets, many people get caught out by not taking up the correct position – as far to the right as possible.

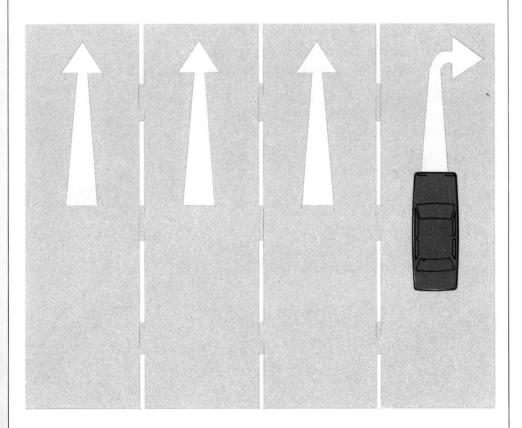

Make sure you are not one of them. At the same time, remember that many drivers are often not aware of this position for turning right, or are just not with it. Look out for them and allow them to get out of your way, if it is safe to do so.

# Roundabouts

The main advantage of roundabouts is that traffic is allowed to flow freely at them. This saves the experienced driver from having to stop and wait when it is not necessary to do so.

The disadvantage of roundabouts, from the learner-driver's point of view, is that you often find that you have to make an *instant* decision – whether to stop or not.

In fact, the decision is a simple *yes* or *no* – *stop* or *continue*. And provided you arrive at the roundabout looking in the proper direction, the decision is usually made for you.

The basic rule which applies to over ninety-nine per cent of round-abouts is that you must **give way to traffic on your right**.

If you have to give way to the left, you will get plenty of warning – usually with **double broken lines**, not single ones.

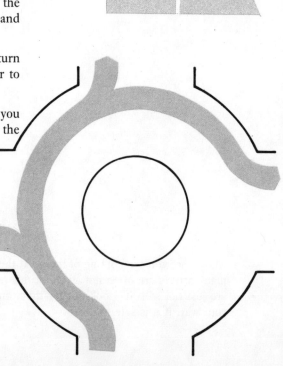

The ideal way to think of a roundabout is to imagine it as a long one-way street, with only left turns available off it.

Your approach to the roundabout will be exactly the same as for any junction.

- You need to remind yourself of the direction you wish to take and position yourself accordingly.

- The further away your own left turn is, the further you can drive over to the right.

- If your left turn is the next one, you should be in the lane nearest to the left *before* you get there.

The overriding principle to be applied at any roundabout is to obey any direction signs or arrows which are given. Then, follow a set pattern – take up a position on approach that suits the exit you wish to take (left for first left, right for furthest exit, etc.).

1 Check your mirrors.

2 Decide when and what signals to give.

3 Carry out your manoeuvre.

- If you intend to take the first exit, you can usually signal *left* into, through and out from the roundabout.

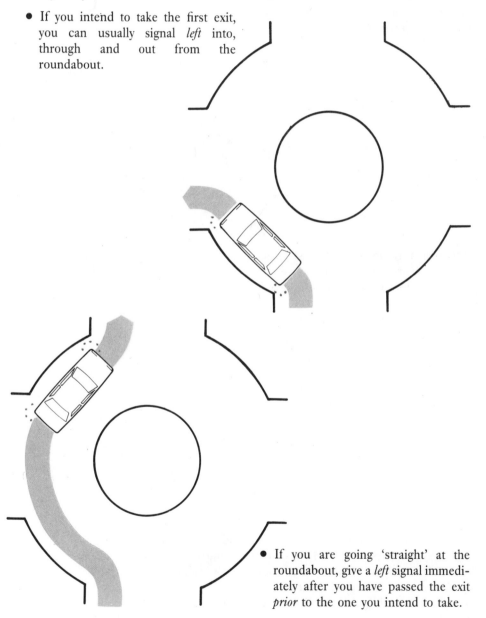

- If you are going 'straight' at the roundabout, give a *left* signal immediately after you have passed the exit *prior* to the one you intend to take.

- If you intend to go 'right' at the roundabout, give a *right* signal on approach, maintain it through the roundabout and then change to a *left* signal at the exit prior to the one you wish to take.

By adopting this sequence of signalling, other drivers will have a reasonably good idea of your intentions – and this is always the purpose of signalling.

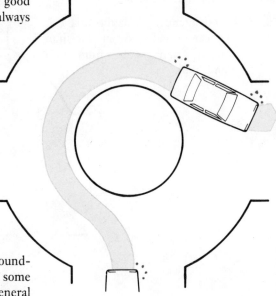

Although this applies to most round-abouts, you are likely to come across some which do not conform to the general pattern of roundabouts – at these, you need to take that extra degree of caution.

One way you need to take extra care is in the use of your mirrors – especially the passenger's side door or wing mirror. You may even find – on some particularly large roundabouts with traffic coming quickly from all directions – that you need to look around to your left or right, as you do when you check your blind spots.

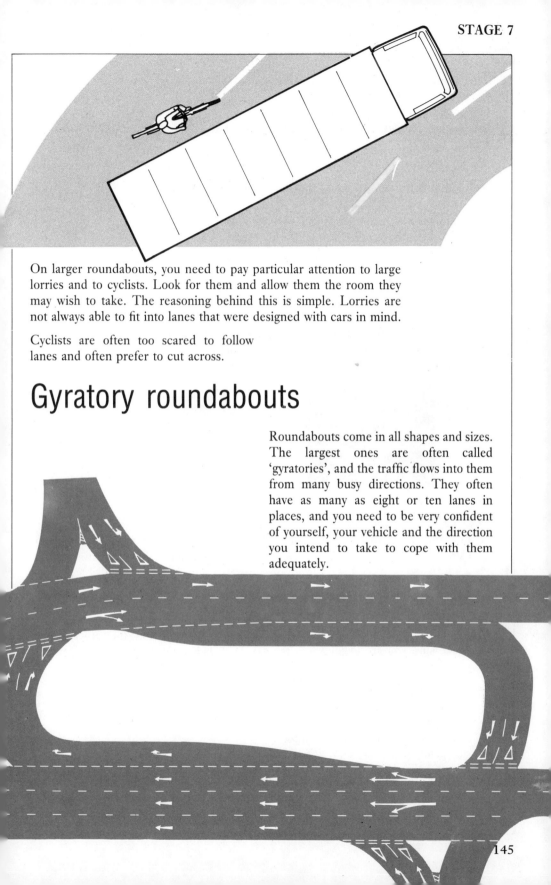

On larger roundabouts, you need to pay particular attention to large lorries and to cyclists. Look for them and allow them the room they may wish to take. The reasoning behind this is simple. Lorries are not always able to fit into lanes that were designed with cars in mind.

Cyclists are often too scared to follow lanes and often prefer to cut across.

# Gyratory roundabouts

Roundabouts come in all shapes and sizes. The largest ones are often called 'gyratories', and the traffic flows into them from many busy directions. They often have as many as eight or ten lanes in places, and you need to be very confident of yourself, your vehicle and the direction you intend to take to cope with them adequately.

145

The best way to learn to cope with gyratory roundabouts is to enter and leave by the first exit for a number of times before you commit yourself to more adventurous routes.

**Sequence to follow at conventional roundabouts**

Conventional roundabouts are usually busy crossroads and multiple junctions which have been turned into roundabouts to help the flow of traffic.

- If you can see your exit on approach, most of your worries are resolved.

- If you cannot see the exit you need, it is usually well signposted for you. Look for the main signpost first and, if you are staying local, look at the secondary sign for local directions.

- Note whether you need to take the first, second or whatever subsequent exit.

- Begin your MSM sequence early – position yourself correctly on approach and adjust your speed to suit the road and traffic.

- Make sure you are looking into the roundabout on approach.

- Make sure you are looking at vehicles entering your vision on your right to see if you can fit safely into any gaps which are presented. If you cannot, stop gently so you do not frighten the drivers behind you.

- If (or when) you do join the traffic stream, travel around the roundabout at whatever is the common speed.

- When you change lanes, make sure you do so only after you have checked that it is safe.

- Do not rely on the other traffic checking before they change lanes.

# Small and mini roundabouts

On the smaller roundabouts – e.g., those that only link three roads or separate a Y junction – you can often see your way clear from some distance back.

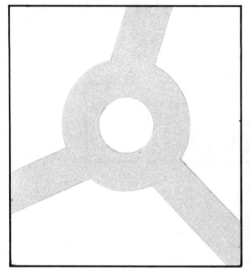

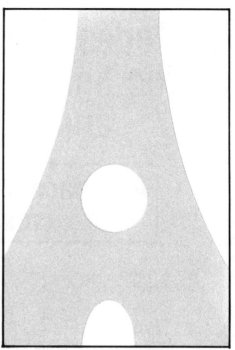

Nevertheless, you should still follow the same sequence on approach and make sure you signal as necessary.

Where the centre of the roundabout is very small indeed – called a mini roundabout – you will see that the centre is either painted on the road surface or is occasionally raised from it like a dustbin lid.

The same rules apply here as with any other roundabout. The exception is that you are allowed to cross the *painted* centre, if it is safer to do so. Where the centre is solid, you must not drive across it.

# STAGE 8

# Pedestrian crossings, traffic lights, box junctions and bus lanes

## Approaching pedestrian crossings

The correct approach to any pedestrian crossing is to regard it as a piece of pavement across the road.

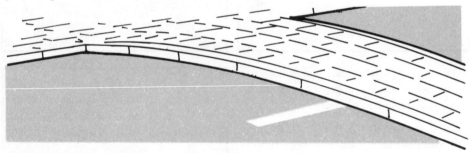

The pedestrians have absolute priority once they are on it.

The main problem, however, is that pedestrians are not subject to the same mechanical rules as cars. Unlike a car, a pedestrian can change speed and direction instantly – and they usually do so just as you've decided that the crossing is safe to use.

It's been established legally that any pedestrian, no matter how he gets there, has absolute priority once he has a foot on the crossing. So your approach to any pedestrian crossing must be to make a positive effort to ensure that *any* pedestrian who can use the crossing is allowed to do so.

But, at the same time, you must also bear in mind that all drivers do not always feel the same way about pedestrians at crossings. So, if you slow down, or stop, you must also inform *anyone* around you who may need to know what you intend to do.

This is where intelligent use of arm signals can help ensure that everyone knows what you are doing. It also helps all the traffic near the crossing to flow smoothly.

Clearly given arm signals show all road users, including pedestrians ahead of you, that you are fully aware of them and that you intend to slow down or stop for the crossing.

Pedestrian crossings fall into two categories:

- controlled
- uncontrolled

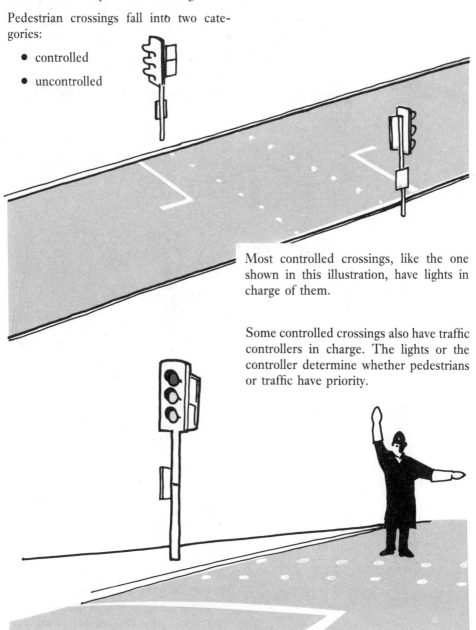

Most controlled crossings, like the one shown in this illustration, have lights in charge of them.

Some controlled crossings also have traffic controllers in charge. The lights or the controller determine whether pedestrians or traffic have priority.

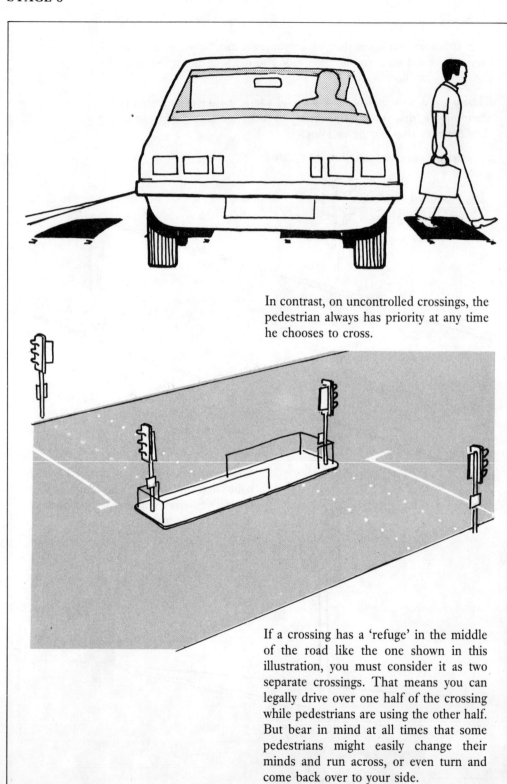

In contrast, on uncontrolled crossings, the pedestrian always has priority at any time he chooses to cross.

If a crossing has a 'refuge' in the middle of the road like the one shown in this illustration, you must consider it as two separate crossings. That means you can legally drive over one half of the crossing while pedestrians are using the other half. But bear in mind at all times that some pedestrians might easily change their minds and run across, or even turn and come back over to your side.

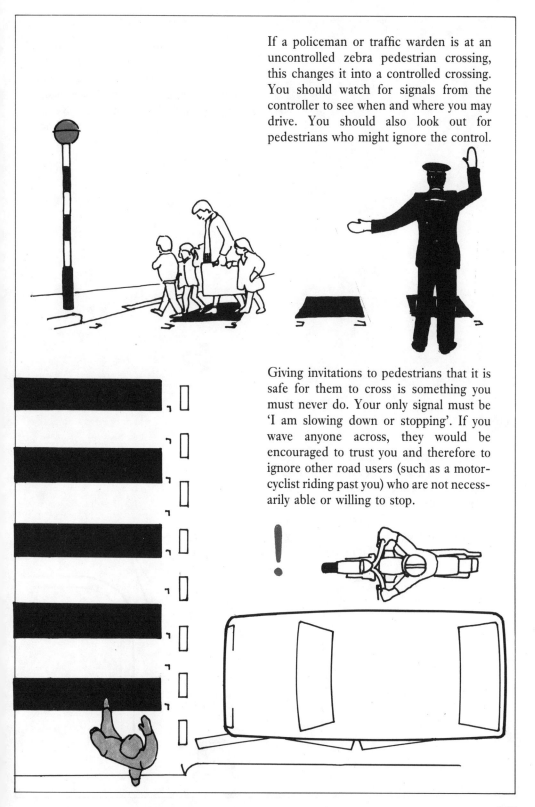

If a policeman or traffic warden is at an uncontrolled zebra pedestrian crossing, this changes it into a controlled crossing. You should watch for signals from the controller to see when and where you may drive. You should also look out for pedestrians who might ignore the control.

Giving invitations to pedestrians that it is safe for them to cross is something you must never do. Your only signal must be 'I am slowing down or stopping'. If you wave anyone across, they would be encouraged to trust you and therefore to ignore other road users (such as a motor-cyclist riding past you) who are not necessarily able or willing to stop.

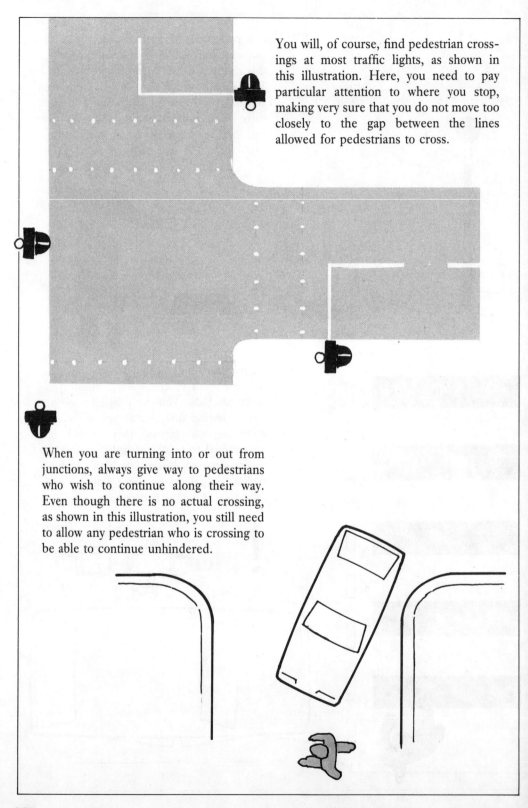

You will, of course, find pedestrian crossings at most traffic lights, as shown in this illustration. Here, you need to pay particular attention to where you stop, making very sure that you do not move too closely to the gap between the lines allowed for pedestrians to cross.

When you are turning into or out from junctions, always give way to pedestrians who wish to continue along their way. Even though there is no actual crossing, as shown in this illustration, you still need to allow any pedestrian who is crossing to be able to continue unhindered.

Most crossings are recognised as zebras, which are distinguished by black and white stripes across the road and belisha beacons.

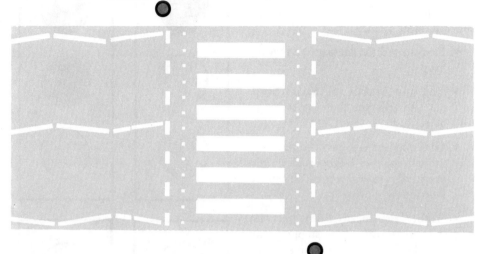

The most important features for you to pay attention to are the zig-zag lines on both sides of the crossing. The length of the zig-zags varies, but is usually about twenty-two metres.

The zig-zags are there to prevent drivers from parking on them and to keep drivers from overtaking others on them. The logic behind the zig-zag lines is to give a clear view of the crossing to all road users approaching it.

No one is permitted to stop within the zig-zag lines except to allow pedestrians to cross. Nor is any vehicle permitted to overtake a leading vehicle on the left-hand lane on the approach, whilst in the area of the zig-zags.

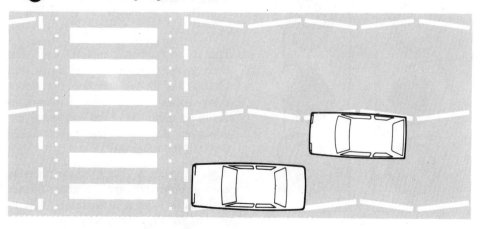

# Traffic lights

Although most people recognise the order in which traffic lights change when they see them, they often read the wrong message from them.

- **Red** is a positive message and means **Stop**.

- **Red and Amber** still means **Stop**, but also tells you that you ought to be ready to move off.

- **Green** means **Go**, but only if the way through the traffic lights is clear, and providing you will not block up the junction by moving forward.

- **Amber** also means **Stop**, but with the proviso that if by stopping you are likely to cause an accident, you may continue. This is the one signal which is most frequently abused.

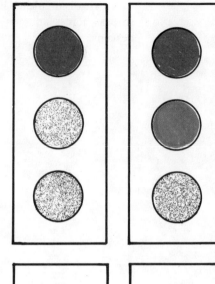

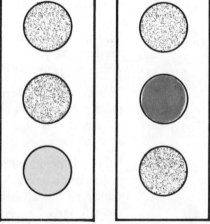

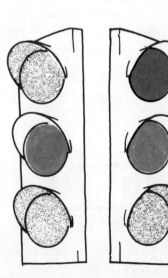

The name 'amber gamblers' has been given to those motorists who try to take advantage of the red and amber or amber alone signals. The problem is shown in this illustration, where red and amber are shown one way at the same time as amber is shown the other way.

What happens is that there are just as many gamblers who try to beat the former as the latter, and it is, therefore, easy to see why so many incidents occur.

Many sets of traffic lights at busy junctions also incorporate **green filter lights**. Their purpose is to allow certain lanes of traffic to move off, while others are held back by a red light.

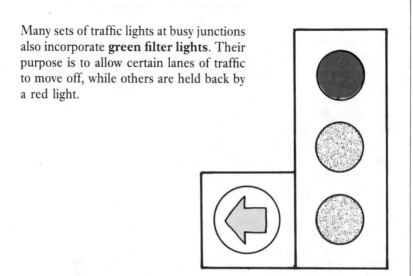

Look out for green filter lights if you are turning yourself, making sure you get in the correct lane. You should also beware of them when you are going straight ahead, making sure you do not get in the wrong lane. Remember – if you *are* in the wrong lane, you are virtually committing yourself to going the wrong way.

The rules for approaching traffic lights are simple. And the hallmark of the skilful driver is one who can arrive at a 'not so busy' set of traffic lights just as the light changes to green.

- If you are turning left, make sure you look well ahead for direction arrows and for filter lights;

- Approach in the correct lane and at the speed most suited to enable you to keep up with other traffic;

- At the same time, adjust your speed down enough to be able to stop safely if the lights change to amber.

- Unless the lights have just gone to green, always expect them to change and be prepared and *willing* to stop when they do so.

- If you approach traffic lights and they are green on approach (something we call 'stale green'), be aware of the fact that they will soon change – it is only a question of time. The correct attitude to take is to make sure that you don't take any chances. You'll also be safer if you look out for other drivers who might be changing their minds (or their lanes) at the last minute.

# Box junctions

A box junction can immediately be recognised by the heavy criss-cross pattern of yellow lines painted across the intersection of some busy roads.

If drivers all used common sense and obeyed the simple traffic light rule for green, which says 'Only go forward if your way is clear', box junctions would not be necessary. But all drivers do not always use their common sense and so we have box junctions. You, therefore, need to learn how they must be used and obeyed.

The rule is that you must not enter an intersection if, by so doing, you will block the junction instead of getting through it. If the junction has a box junction painted on it, entering it is not only pointless, but illegal.

So when you come across a junction – usually controlled by traffic lights – with the yellow box markings in it, you must not drive on to the yellow markings unless you can drive beyond them and clear the junction.

The only exception is if you intend to turn right and the only thing which prevents you from completing the turn is the traffic coming towards you. In this case, you *are* allowed to wait in the box, provided that when you enter it, you are sure that you will be able to clear the junction completely once the lights change or the oncoming traffic ceases.

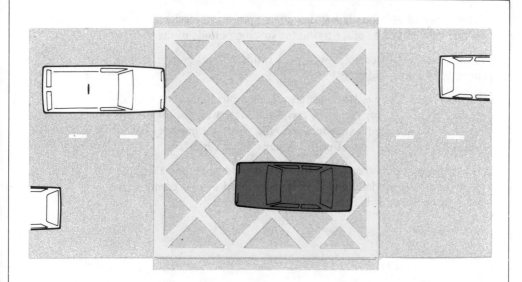

Learners (and many experienced drivers) often worry about whether this means only one car may enter a box junction at a time when turning right. The answer is:

- If you are sure that you (as the second or even third vehicle) will be able to leave the box safely when the lights change, you are entitled to enter the box.

- If you are not sure, do not enter it.

- You also need to make sure that by waiting in the box, you are not preventing other traffic from turning the other way.

# Bus lanes

While driving through most towns, it is difficult *not* to come across a bus lane.

There are two factors to take into account about bus lanes:

1 The first, and most obvious, is that the sign indicating the presence of a bus lane also indicates those vehicles which are allowed to use them. Quite often, they also allow taxis and bicycles.

2 The second factor is the duration or timing of the restriction on the lane, and this is also indicated on the sign. A few bus lanes are only for the use of buses and some are in use twenty-four hours a day.

But the majority of bus lanes also allow taxis and bicycles in them and are only closed to other traffic for specific periods of the day.

These times usually coincide with peak traffic periods going into and out of busy towns and cities.

In a few cases, the bus lanes are also 'contra-flow', meaning that all the traffic lanes in any one road travel the same way, except for the bus lane. To all intents and purposes, the road is a one-way street, except for the single lane of traffic designated as a bus lane.

It is separated from other traffic by a broad solid white line along the whole length of the lane and is only to be used in that contra-flow direction by buses. It is banned to all other traffic.

Other bus lanes occur where the left-hand lane of a two- or three-lane road is earmarked for buses (and taxis/cycles as well) and is marked by a broad solid white line along the length of the road, but the traffic flow is with the normal traffic.

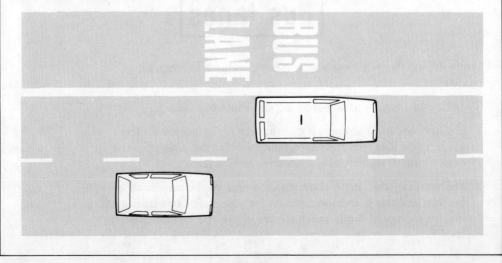

For ordinary motorists, there is more danger attached to the use of this 'with traffic flow' bus lane than with contra-flow lanes.

When driving along in a lane parallel to and in the same direction as a bus lane being used, you need to be especially careful of other motorists who either forget or disregard the rules.

This can be extremely annoying at the end of a bus lane when you wish to join that part of the road, only to find that it is already full of non-bus traffic.

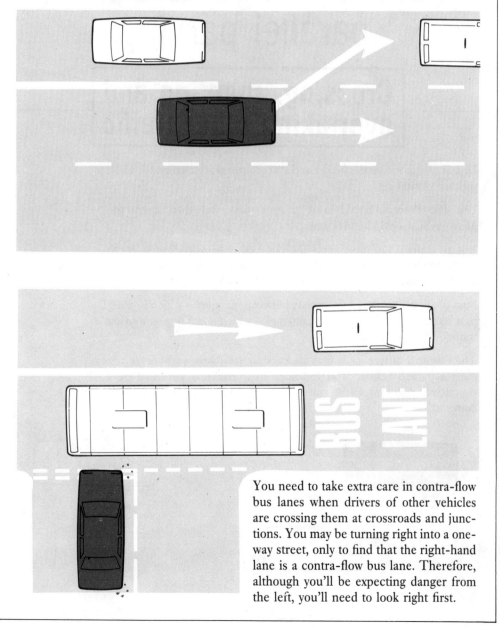

You need to take extra care in contra-flow bus lanes when drivers of other vehicles are crossing them at crossroads and junctions. You may be turning right into a one-way street, only to find that the right-hand lane is a contra-flow bus lane. Therefore, although you'll be expecting danger from the left, you'll need to look right first.

# Crossing, meeting and overtaking other traffic, dual carriageways and parallel parking

## Crossing, meeting and overtaking other traffic

One occasion where the MSM and PSL routines are changed is when you are overtaking.

Use the Position-Speed-Look routine first and then apply the Mirrors-Signal-Manoeuvre one.

But, of course, you must apply the same exact principles of safety to overtaking as to any other form of driving – only do it when you are absolutely sure it is safe to complete the entire manoeuvre.

First of all, we need to differentiate between 'passing' – which is going past stationary traffic – and 'overtaking' – which is going past moving traffic in the same direction.

The essential difference is that the need to 'pass' arises whenever you meet a parked vehicle. But the need to overtake is governed by a completely different set of rules, the main one being 'Why are you doing it?'

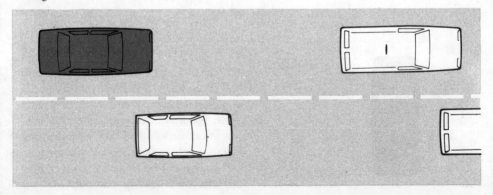

- Why do you need to overtake in the first place?

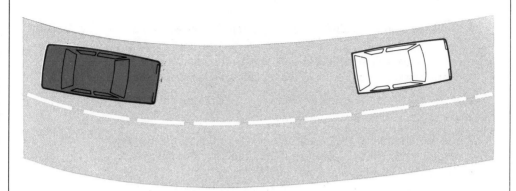

- Would you be safer by staying behind the vehicle you wish to go past?

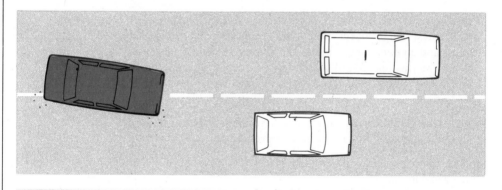

- Would you be better off by getting past the vehicle at the most suitable moment?

The most suitable time is on a dual carriageway when the vehicle you are overtaking is travelling at least twenty m.p.h. slower than you.

*The Highway Code* highlights a number of places where it is not suitable to overtake and, in some of them, illegal to do so.

**How much time do you have to overtake?**

- If you have a speed difference of ten m.p.h., you will need at least ten seconds to overtake safely. And in that time, an oncoming vehicle travelling at sixty m.p.h. will have covered 270 metres towards you, and often on a collision course with you.

- If you have a speed difference of twenty m.p.h., you will require five seconds to get past safely.

- But if you have a difference of only five m.p.h., you would require at least twenty seconds. In that time, the oncoming sixty m.p.h. vehicle will have covered 536 metres; and if you are travelling at the same speed, you would also travel 536 metres. Measure out 1072 metres sometime and surprise yourself.

# Crossing other traffic

Crossing other traffic mainly occurs when you are turning right. The greatest danger occurs when you are turning right into a side turning and an oncoming vehicle is an indeterminate distance away. Once more, his speed and the distance between you are the key factors. And always remember that you have no control over his speed at all.

Three-lane single-carriageway roads have often been regarded as the least suitable of all our roads for travelling on.

In fact, they can be thought of as having three separate lanes:

- the lane for you, called 'our side'

- the lane for oncoming traffic, called 'their side'

- the middle lane, for those who wish to hog their way through – called 'sui-cide'

The greatest possible care must always be taken when meeting, crossing the path of or overtaking any other vehicle at any time.

The secret of good, safe and successful overtaking is always to hang back far enough behind the preceding vehicle, so that you can pull out, assess the situation, accelerate quickly and then decide to get past. Avoid getting too close, then picking up speed and pulling out all at the same time so that you are overtaking too slowly.

# Dual carriageways

Many main roads have keep-left bollards in them at junctions like the one shown in this illustration.

Their purpose is to make sure that the traffic knows where the middle of the road is.

Main roads which have a central reservation right through them are called **dual carriageways**, like the one shown in this illustration.

Their intended purpose is to make the roads safer and to allow traffic to travel at higher speeds. But this, in itself, can create other problems associated with driving at high speeds.

Your **Mirrors – Signal – Manoeuvre** procedure is therefore even more important for you to follow than on single carriageway roads. This is because most dual carriageways allow two or more lanes of traffic travelling at high speeds in both directions and overtaking is much more common.

Turning right from a dual carriageway can be just as simple as a normal right turn. But, you must always remember to wait in a safe position and be aware of the fact that the speed of oncoming traffic might be much higher than you expect.

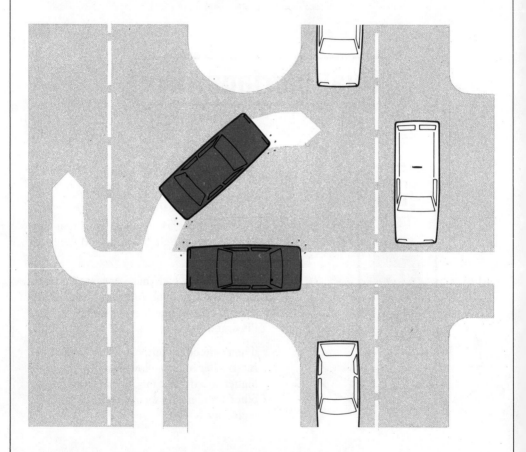

When you are turning right on to a dual carriageway, remember, in effect, you are crossing *two* roads.

- Regard the first road as a one-way street on your right.

- Regard the second as a one-way street on the left.

- You may be able to wait in the middle, but only if you can do so without inconveniencing any other road user.

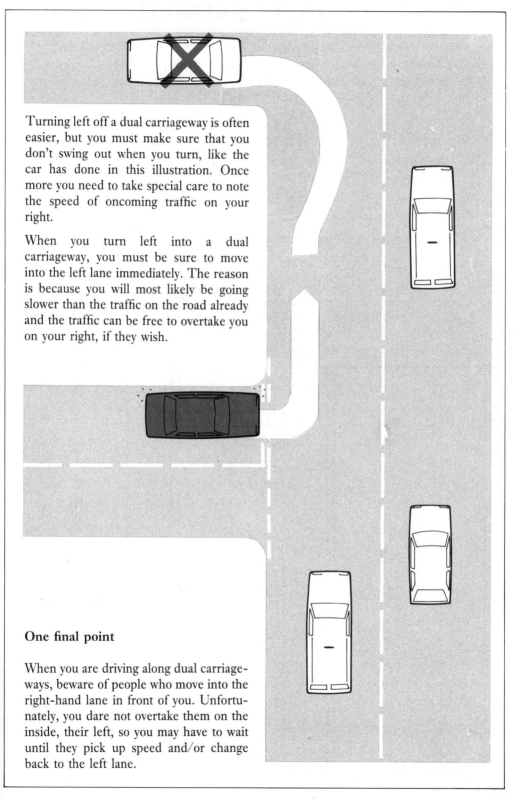

Turning left off a dual carriageway is often easier, but you must make sure that you don't swing out when you turn, like the car has done in this illustration. Once more you need to take special care to note the speed of oncoming traffic on your right.

When you turn left into a dual carriageway, you must be sure to move into the left lane immediately. The reason is because you will most likely be going slower than the traffic on the road already and the traffic can be free to overtake you on your right, if they wish.

### One final point

When you are driving along dual carriageways, beware of people who move into the right-hand lane in front of you. Unfortunately, you dare not overtake them on the inside, their left, so you may have to wait until they pick up speed and/or change back to the left lane.

# Parallel parking

Parallel parking, or parking at the kerb, is one of those skills that many learners do not attempt. They think it is more difficult than it is, and, because it is usually not required for the test, they leave it until later.

There are two flaws to this argument.

1 It is no more difficult to do than any other form of reversing and requires exactly the same skills.

2 You may very well have to do this exercise on the test, especially if there is no car park at the test centre.

Parallel parking is only an extension of 'reversing around the corner'.

The sequence to carry it out is simple:

- Drive along until you see a gap between parked cars (e.g., at a meter) which is large enough for you. Two car lengths is ideal for your first attempt; a car and a half is simple for experienced drivers; a car and a third is tight; and a car and a quarter is only for the skilled, but a target for all drivers.

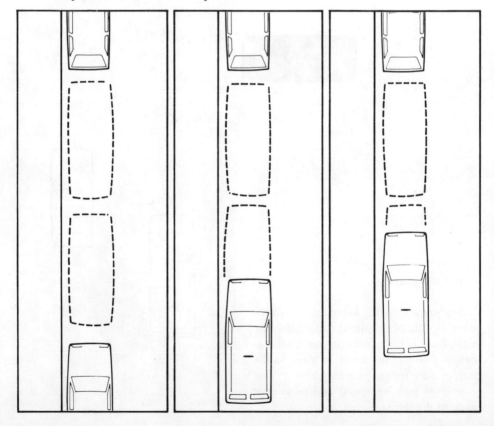

- Stop alongside the first car until the traffic is clear enough for you to start the parallel parking exercise.

- Then move forward alongside the second car, stop and select reverse gear. This has the advantage of showing other traffic your reversing lights.

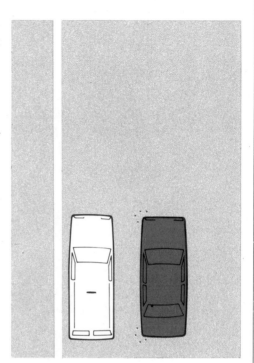

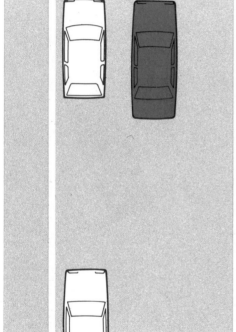

- When it is clear all around you, start to reverse, turning your steering wheel quickly and fully to the left. This has the effect of pushing the rear wheels into the gap and the front wheels out into the road.

- It is *essential*, therefore, to look all around the front immediately *before* you do this.

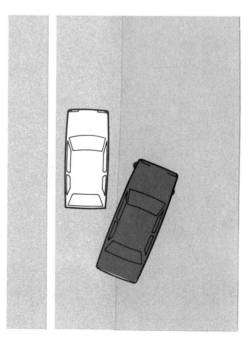

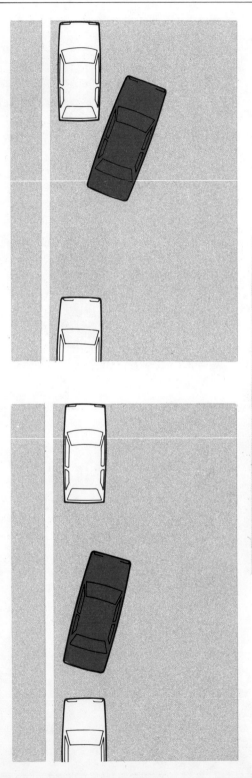

- Aim the rear of your car towards the front of the car behind you.

- Correct your steering by turning the wheel back again, so that you continue to steer towards the front of the car.

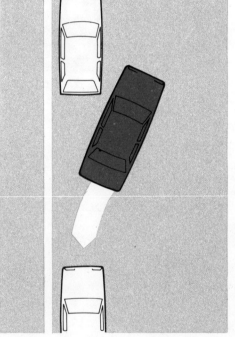

- As soon as your front is clear of the other car, turn your steering wheel to the right, quickly and fully, once more.

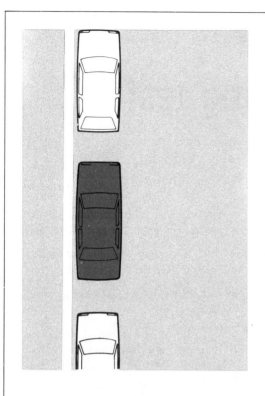

- Then, as you aim towards the car behind, correct the steering quickly to the straight-ahead position once more. You will know you are straight ahead because you'll be aiming squarely at that car.

# Practice

Practise the exercise first with only one car – the one behind you – and you can forget any worries about the one ahead.

Only practise with two cars when you are confident that you can totally ignore the leading car when you steer.

As with all reversing, you must look at what you want to hit – in this case, the car behind you. (Only try to manage to stop before you actually make contact!)

# The driving test

## The requirements

The requirements for the Department of Transport driving test are explained generally in the DL68 booklet *Your Driving Test*, available free with your driving licence or from your instructor. In general, you need to show the examiner that you are a competent driver who can handle your vehicle safely, show courtesy and consideration for other road users and observe *The Highway Code*.

The driving test application form DL26 or DL26M (available from any post office) also defines the requirements in more detail.

You must be able to:

- show you are fully conversant with *The Highway Code*

- demonstrate you are competent to drive without danger to others and that you show consideration for other road users at all times

- read a number plate at the required distance of sixty-seven feet or seventy-five feet

- start the engine safely

- move away safely

- overtake, meet and cross the path of other traffic correctly and safely

- turn right and left correctly and with safety

- stop safely in an emergency and stop normally in a suitable part of the road

- drive backwards and enter a limited opening either to the right or the left

- cause the vehicle to face the opposite direction using forward and reverse gears

- indicate your intentions by giving suitable signals – clearly and unmistakably

- act correctly and promptly on all signals given by signs and traffic controllers, and take appropriate action on signs given by other road users

Everything you learn when you have your driving lessons is designed to ensure that you are being correctly prepared for some or all of the above requirements. It is in your own interest to see that you understand exactly how you do each of them and to find out from your instructor how well you do them.

The number of lessons you will need to pass your test does, of course, vary depending on a number of factors; but the number of lessons is reduced once you know precisely what you have to do to pass.

An excellent way to find out whether you are ready for your test is to take the test in my other book, *Are You Ready For Your*

*Driving Test?* (Pan Books, 1983). It has already helped over 65,000 learner-drivers to pass their tests.

Most importantly, on the test you must be able to

- demonstrate that you are competent to drive without danger to others

- show consideration for other road users at all times

The first two paragraphs in the DL68 are concerned with the need to be competent and the third paragraph tells you to make sure that you have good instruction – and enough of it. If you are properly prepared you will pass the test first time.

Like the examiners, your instructor has been trained on the methods used in the DL68, *The Highway Code* and the DPT manual *Driving*. His training course follows exactly the same pattern as that of an examiner and he knows exactly what the examiner expects to see on the test.

The main thing to remember is that a competent driver is one who performs all the correct actions from habit and not by remembering that he is taking a driving test and therefore needs to do special things for the examiner.

Obviously, one of the first signs of competence is to make certain that your health and eyesight are both good enough to meet the requirements of the test. You must be able to read a number plate (seven-figure letters) at sixty-seven feet, or one with six-figure letters at seventy-five feet.

If you need to wear glasses to read the number plates, you must also wear glasses every time that you drive.

You must not be under the influence of drink or drugs during the test or at any time that you drive; if you are taking any tablets or medication, make sure that your doctor agrees they are safe to take while you are driving.

Also remember that taking your test is a stressful situation and you need to concentrate fully at all times on the road ahead and the conditions around you. You cannot do this if you are unwell or if you have any private or domestic worries which might affect your judgement or capabilities. Once more, if you feel you may be affected, please discuss it with your instructor.

# Skills and standards

During your course of driving lessons leading up to your driving test, you will be required to perform a variety of skills; and it is important that you are able to recognise the precise standard required for each of these skills.

*You must be able to*

| | |
|---|---|
| Safety checks | Understand and put into practice the necessary safety checks to ensure a safe drive, every time. |
| Starting, steering and stopping | Move off from rest, follow a safety line correctly and bring your car to rest smoothly at any given point, without any undue effort. |
| Moving off | Move off and make suitable progress with regard to road and traffic conditions, so as not to cause any unnecessary hold-ups with the traffic flow. |
| Gear changing | Change gears correctly and smoothly, with good timing and smooth action. You must not jerk the car, nor cause any loss of speed through your gear changes. |
| Car controls | Make adequate use of all the car's controls correctly, without harshness or fierceness, especially when making use of more than one control at once; you must be able to coordinate the use of the car's controls correctly and at all times. |
| Mirrors | Make effective use of the mirrors fitted to the car and make full use of the Mirrors – Signal – Manoeuvre routine each time you encounter any hazard or contemplate a change of speed or direction. |
| Emergency stop | Stop the car quickly, but safely, under full control, not only in a simulated emergency, but when any real emergency situation arises. |
| Corners | Approach bends, corners, junctions and turnings at the correct speed, and apply the necessary MSM and PSL routines. |

| | |
|---|---|
| Positioning generally | Follow a safety line at all times, regardless of changes of speed and direction; when traffic situations dictate, you must be able to keep slow enough to allow a closer path. |
| Junctions and crossroads | Deal successfully with each type of right and left turns into and out of major roads; you must also be able to decide correctly each time you come to a junction or a crossroad whether to stop or proceed safely. |
| Meeting, overtaking and crossing other traffic | Judge correctly the speed and distance of all other traffic and road users so that you can meet them safely, cross their path safely and, where necessary, overtake them and get back into your correct safety line – without causing any other road user to brake or swerve to avoid you. |
| Pedestrian crossings | Negotiate pedestrian crossings of all types and recognise the legal implications and requirements on approach and while crossing them; you must allow pedestrians any necessary priority, without being a danger to any other following or oncoming traffic. |
| Manoeuvres | Reverse in a straight line, to the right and to the left – around corners and into limited openings – without any danger or inconvenience to any other road users. |
| | Turn the car around in the road safely and methodically, without inconvenience to any other road users. |
| | Park the car at the kerbside in reverse gear safely and correctly without any inconvenience or danger to any other road users. |
| Anticipation | Plan your driving so that all your actions are smooth and premeditated; you must also be aware of any dangerous situations before they get out of hand and be able to cope with them correctly. |

*The Highway Code*

Answer any question based on the contents of *The Highway Code*, or the DL68, or any motoring matters.

# The driving test

So much for the requirements, skills and standards. Now to the practical part of the driving test, which lasts for about thirty minutes. In this time, the examiner will follow a pre-determined route and check all the items that need to be tested.

He will use a special marking sheet called a DL25 Driving Test Report to note any errors which you might make.

The abbreviations in the report represent the paragraph headings in the DL68 booklet *Your Driving Test.*

During the test, he will also classify your errors into three categories:

- minor
- serious
- dangerous

For those candidates who fail, the examiner will mark the serious and dangerous errors on a Statement of Failure form.

Department of Transport

**Driving Test Report**

Centre

Date / /

Candidate's full name

Name of School (where known)

Particulars of vehicle  P  C  S   Make

Type

Reg Mark

Group   Year   19

| | | | | | | | | |
|---|---|---|---|---|---|---|---|---|
| FET | 1 | MIR SIG | 9 | J SP + | 14 |
| HC | 2 | DIR | 9 | OBS | 14 |
| | | ST | 9 | POSR | 14 |
| PRE | 3 | ROB SIG | 9 | POSL | 14 |
| | | DIR | 9 | RCC | 14 |
| ACC | 4 | ST | 9 | | |
| CL | 4 | | | OT | 15 |
| G | 4 | SIG O | 10 | MAT | 15 |
| F.BR | 4 | W | 10 | CAT | 15 |
| H.BR | 4 | L | 10 | POSN | 16 |
| ST | 4 | | | | |
| | | SNS ST | 11 | SH.V | 17 |
| MO PRE | 5 | DIR | 11 | | |
| CON | 5 | NE | 11 | PX | 18 |
| | | RM | 11 | NS | 19 |
| ES | 6 | TRA L | 11 | | |
| FR.BR | 6 | CON | 11 | AA PED | 20 |
| RV CON | 7 | SIG ORU | 11 | CYC | 20 |
| OBS | 7 | | | DRI | 20 |
| | | PRO + | 12 | | |
| TR CON | 8 | | | ETA V | |
| OBS | 8 | PRO − | 13 | P | |

DL25 (1990)

Department of Transport
ROAD TRAFFIC ACT 1972

Test Centre:

**Statement of Failure to Pass Test of Competence to Drive**     X 482422

Name .....................................................................................

has this day been examined and has failed to pass the test of competence to drive prescribed for the purposes of section 85 of the Road Traffic Act 1972.

Date .................

*Authorised by the Minister of Transport to conduct tests*

Examiners have regard to the items listed below in deciding whether a candidate is competent to drive. The matters needing special attention are marked for your information and assistance and should be studied in detail. (See Note 1 overleaf)

1. ☐ Comply with the requirements of the eyesight test.
2. ☐ Know the Highway Code.
3. ☐ Take proper precautions before starting the engine.
4. ☐ Make proper use of accelerator/clutch/gears/footbrake/handbrake/steering.
5. ☐ Move away/safely/under control.
6. ☐ Stop the vehicle in an emergency/promptly/under control/making proper use of front brake.
7. ☐ Reverse into a limited opening either to the right or left/under control/with due regard for other road users.
8. ☐ Turn round by means of forward and reverse gears/under control/with due regard for other road users.
9. ☐ Make effective use of mirror(s) well before } Take effective rear observation well before } signalling/changing direction/slowing down or stopping.
10. ☐ Give signals/where necessary/correctly/in good time.
11. ☐ Take prompt and appropriate action on all/traffic signs/road markings/traffic lights/signals given by traffic controllers/other road users.
12. ☐ Exercise proper care in the use of speed.
13. ☐ Make progress by/driving at a speed appropriate to the road and traffic conditions/avoiding undue hesitancy.
14. ☐ Act properly at road junctions:-
    - regulate speed correctly on approach;
    - take effective observation before emerging;
    - position the vehicle correctly/before turning right/before turning left;
    - avoid cutting right hand corners.
15. ☐ Overtake/meet/cross the path of/other vehicles safely.
16. ☐ Position the vehicle correctly during normal driving.
17. ☐ Allow adequate clearance to stationary vehicles.
18. ☐ Take appropriate action at pedestrian crossings.
19. ☐ Select a safe position for normal stops.
20. ☐ Show awareness and anticipation of the actions of/pedestrians/cyclists/drivers.

DRIVING EXAMINERS ARE NOT PERMITTED TO DISCUSS DETAILS OF THE TEST     SEE GUIDANCE NOTES OVERLEAF

51-2988 1/83 OBR LTD

DL 24
6/80

As you can see, each error is underlined so that the candidate can see where he went wrong, like, for example, Item 4 – not making proper use of the accelerator, gears and steering. The examiner then hands this form to the candidate with the suggestion that further study of the underlined items will help next time.

Quite often the examiner will also issue another copy of the DL68 booklet *Your Driving Test* which, if read carefully, holds the clue as to what you have to do in order to have your driving assessed as competent.

### Phase 1

The examiner meets and greets the candidate. A lot of time is spent during the training of examiners to ensure that they meet test candidates correctly and put them at ease, without seeming to be too friendly.

He requires you to sign his daily journal which serves as his receipt from you for the driving test to be conducted.

He also compares your signature on the journal with that on your driving test application form. If necessary, he can also compare these two signatures with the one on your provisional driving licence.

The Statement of Failure form, like the examiner's marking sheet, is simply a list of the paragraph headings in the booklet – covering all the items to be tested.

Therefore, as a driving test candidate, you never need to worry about what the examiner is writing, or what the markings mean on his 'secret' sheet. The only information you need is written for you in the DL68 booklet.

To help the examiner conduct the test in an organised way, it is broken down into a series of five phases.

Here is what the examiner actually says to you:

'Good morning ... Would you sign against your name, please?'

You are then asked to lead the way to your car and, at the same time, the examiner will ask about any disabilities you might have.

'Will you lead the way to your vehicle, please. Have you any physical disability that isn't declared on your application?'

This is not a trick, merely a means to allow you to confirm to the examiner that you understand that 'disabled drivers' can be tested too. It is also a means to ensure that, if you have any disability, the examiner knows what it is.

Once outside, he will ask you to identify your car and then ask you to read the registration number of a car just beyond the required distance of sixty-seven or seventy-five feet.

The examiner will then say, 'Will you get into your car, please?' At the same time, he will make a note about certain things about your car, the type and model, etc.

### Phase 2

Phase 2 is called the 'natural drive' and begins with the examiner explaining to you how the test will be conducted and how he will give his directions.

'I shall ask you to follow the road ahead, or as direction signs indicate, unless I want you to turn. I'll tell you which way in good time. Move off when you're ready, please.'

While you are driving along the test route, his general directions will be restricted to set phrases such as the following:

'Drive on when you're ready, please.'

'Would you pull up on the left at a convenient place, please.'

'Pull up along here just before that street lamp, please.'

'Take the next road on the right/left, please.'

'Will you take the second road on the right/left, please.'

(If there is likely to be any doubt, he may add, 'This is the first.')

'Take the road to the right/left at the end, please.'

At roundabouts, he will say:

'At the roundabout, take the next road off the left, please.'

'At the roundabout take the road leading off to the right, please.'

'At the roundabout follow the road ahead, please.'

(Note: these instructions will not be appropriate at all roundabouts; therefore the wording may vary to suit the circumstances.)

Having been told by the examiner to move off when you are ready, you can now concentrate on the driving task ahead; but the examiner has a number of things which he must do. He must complete certain entries on his marking sheet, like, for example, more details of the vehicle or car, a description of the candidate and the route chosen.

For this reason and also to allow you to settle down, minor errors are usually disregarded in the first few minutes of this second phase of the test. So, if you see the examiner writing on his marking sheet, you now know that he is not making notes about your errors, but rather, filling in the details required of him.

## Phase 3

After a while, when the quieter roads have been reached, the examiner will check your ability to cope with a number of set manoeuvres. The first of these is nearly always the emergency stop – which begins the third phase of the test.

'Very shortly I shall ask you to stop as in an emergency, the signal will be like this' (and he will demonstrate).

'When I do that, I want you to stop immediately and under full control, as though a child had run off the pavement.'

When you have moved off again, and usually in the course of the next few roads, he will say 'STOP' and, at the same time, strike the windscreen with his book; he then expects you to demonstrate how you would stop 'as in an emergency'.

The only time he would not specially test this exercise would be if a genuine 'emergency' had arisen during the test and you had coped with it successfully.

After the car has stopped and you have applied the handbrake and selected neutral, the examiner will then add:

'Thank you, I shan't ask you to carry out that exercise again.'

You can now see why, in normal driving, he does not use the phrase 'stopping' the car; but rather, the phrase 'pulling up'.

## Phase 4

The examiner now moves on to Phase 4, the 'body of the test'. Items to be tested include:

- Reversing to the left (although reversing to the right is usually the alternative for vans, etc.).

- Turning the car round by forward and reverse gears.

- Moving the car away from the side of the kerb at an angle.

The wording for the reverse begins when the examiner asks you to pull up *before* a road on the left:

'This road on the left is the one I should like you to reverse into. Drive past it and stop; then back in and continue to drive in reverse gear for some distance, keeping reasonably close to the kerb.'

For the turn-in-the-road he will say:

'Would you pull up on the left just past the ... please. I'd like you to turn your car round in the road, to face the opposite direction, using forward and reverse gears. Try not to touch the kerb when you're turning.'

For moving away from the kerb at an angle, he will say:

'Pull up on the left, just before you get to the stationary vehicle...' (and if necessary '...Leave enough room to move away.')

## Phase 5

After these manoeuvres have been completed, the test continues, usually in a stretch of busier traffic, until the examiner asks you to bring the car back to the Test Centre.

There, he will carry out the fifth and final phase of the driving test: questions on *The Highway Code* and other motoring matters.

It is worth stressing that the examiner has actually tested *The Highway Code* and the way in which you have applied the rules of the code all through the driving test; but he still needs to ask you a series of questions to confirm any views formed during the driving itself, and to test your knowledge of items not tested (such as night driving, bad weather, motorways and car maintenance.)

He would normally ask you about five questions and to identify about six traffic signs. For example:

1 'What is the meaning of the amber traffic light on its own?'

2 'When may you overtake a vehicle on the left?'

3 'What particular care should be taken when parking a car at night?'

4 'What do you understand by the double white lines down the middle of the road?'

5 'When are you allowed to filter?'

# Pass or fail

Your test is now concluded.

If you pass, the examiner's words are most welcome:

'That is the end of the test and I'm pleased to be able to tell you that you've passed. Will you sign and put your address here on this pass certificate, please? Make sure you send this off when you apply to change your driving licence. Thank you. Good morning.'

But, of course, he does sometimes need to say:

'That's the end of the test. I'm sorry you haven't passed, but your driving hasn't reached the required standard. If you'll give me a few moments, I'll help you by marking the points to which you should give special attention. Thank you. Good morning.'

It is a good idea for you to understand how the examiner arrives at the decision he makes. The simple answer is that it is *you* that makes the decision for him. During the drive, which is around a predetermined and approved route, he will notice every piece of driving that you do. He will assess each decision which you make and, remembering his own training, will look for every departure from a standard of safe driving which you make.

He has been trained to note every aspect of the drive and, in the light of the error made and the circumstances surrounding the error, decides whether it is a minor error or a more serious one. During his training, the examiner is given precise guidelines to follow in deciding whether the error is minor or serious.

'If, during the drive, this were to be the only mistake that the candidate made, would you assess it as serious or not?'

- 'If yes, then the error is marked accordingly, as serious or dangerous. And any one serious or dangerous error would be sufficient to fail the driving test.'

- 'If the answer was "no", then the error is regarded as a minor error and although it may be marked on his sheet as such, this would not fail the candidate even if the same error was repeated, or other minor errors made as well.'

Each error is marked into one of the boxes on his Driving Test Report *as it is made.* Each item on the report is then detailed in full on the 'failure sheet' and this, you will remember, is described in even more detail in the DL68 booklet *Your Driving Test*, which every learner-driver is given at the beginning of their lessons. The examiner only marks those items on the candidate's failure sheet which he initially assessed as 'serious or dangerous'. Therefore, *every* item on the failure sheet is an important one for drivers to study before retaking the test.

# STAGE 11

# Driving at night, in adverse weather and on motorways

## Driving at night

Everything that has been said about driving in the daytime applies to driving at night – with one very important additional rule: to be safe, you must always be able to stop safely in the distance that you can see ahead.

This rule also applies in the daytime, but is sometimes neglected. You cannot, and dare not, neglect it at night.

- If you cannot see ahead, you must not go.

- If you can only see a little way ahead, you need to drive slowly enough to be able to stop safely in that distance.

### Visibility at night

When you are driving at night, on dipped headlights and on unlighted roads, the throw of your dipped beam is only about forty or fifty feet. Anything beyond that distance is out of your visibility and could be the death of you. The danger is not only from pedestrians, cyclists without lights, or parked cars; it might also be a full skip or a broken-down lorry.

When you hit any of these at speed, they hardly move at all and your car will stop . . . dead.

On main beam, you will find that your visibility is much better – but only in a straight line ahead. You will still have blind spots, either side of the headlight beams, which can be worrying if you are on a bending road.

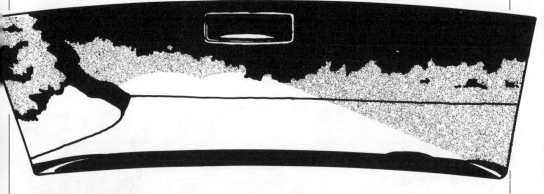

Also, should you need to dip your lights quickly because of an oncoming vehicle, you are suddenly reduced to the 'dipped beam' distance again.

A useful tip for night-time driving is to follow another vehicle travelling at a safe speed, at a reasonable distance behind. That way, you get the benefit of using its lights too, to give yourself a better distance in which to plan your driving.

Remember that distance and speed both work together in relation to the all-important need for 'time'. It is lack of time which causes most people to be incapable of taking the correct action. Time can always be achieved by travelling slower.

### Overtaking at night

Overtaking at night is also much more fraught with potential danger. Unless the roads are well lit, or if they are dark, you know they are straight for at least twenty to thirty seconds' driving time: *do not overtake* – it is not a safe manoeuvre.

Even on dual carriageways, you need to take extra care when overtaking at night.

Motorways are safer, however, because you know they are straight and, by careful and judicious use of the centre and overtaking lanes, you can overtake quickly and safely in the dark.

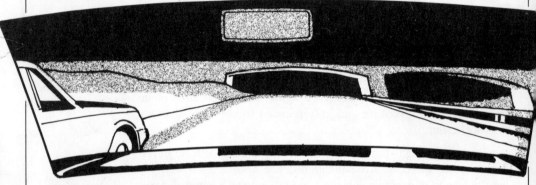

If the road ahead is clear and you are not likely to dazzle traffic on the opposite carriageway, you can use your main headlights once you are alongside the vehicle you are overtaking.

### Using 'parking' lights

If you are driving around built-up areas – even where the street lighting is good – be particularly careful about using 'side' (or, as they should be called, 'parking') lights.

- Remember that one of the main purposes of using lights at night is to warn other people that you are there.

- If you are only using very dim parking lights, it is not always apparent that you are there, or that you are moving.

- Remember, too, that parking at night requires you to think:

  *Would lights be helpful?

  *If you leave them switched off, is it legal?

  *Is anyone likely to find your car an obstacle – especially if the street lights which are on when you leave the car could be switched off later on?

**Benefits of night driving**

There are, of course, benefits in driving at night.

- You usually find less traffic and fewer holdups.

If you decide to drive at night to get a good start to your holidays, remember that night-time is meant for sleeping and make sure you are not tired.

If, for any reason, you feel yourself wanting to nod off, there is only one answer: get off the road as soon as you can. Park, doze and, when you are sure you've recovered, think about continuing.

Never drive if you are in danger of nodding off. In one second, you'll travel nearly ninety feet at sixty m.p.h. – and that could be straight into the oncoming traffic.

# Driving in adverse weather

Anyone who learns to drive in Britain and takes the normal amount of time to learn will certainly find that, during the course of their lessons, they experience most kinds of weather.

Nevertheless, there are certain weather conditions which could take you by surprise.

## Heavy rain

A sudden torrential rainfall can happen at any time – often at the height of a spell of dry, baking-hot days. The pressure builds up and lightning and thunder are the prelude to a really heavy rain. The windscreen wipers simply cannot cope because there is as much water behind each blade as in front.

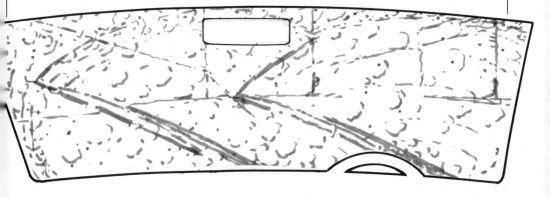

There is only one thing to do. Check your rear-view mirrors, brake gently and either crawl along at a snail's pace or stop. The traffic conditions will dictate which option is better.

Because these sort of showers don't last for long, it is well worth waiting until they are over. You certainly cannot maintain any degree of normal progress during the storm.

Don't be frightened by lightning. While in your car, you are probably safer than anywhere else. And if you can hear the thunder, you know that particular lightning strike has missed you.

# Snow and ice

Snow and ice are other weather conditions which can make driving more difficult. If you drive sensibly, the danger in most cases is not so much what *you* do, but what *other road users* might do to you.

So, once more, your approach must be: drive slower and make certain you are able to stop safely in the distance you *know* to be safe.

If anyone wishes to perform acrobatics, whether in a car or even on a bicycle, slow down so that you can cope with their antics.

Try to avoid stopping on icy and snowy roads because it is often more difficult to start to move off than it is to keep moving.

The extra rule to bear in mind for all icy roads is a simple one:

*You have NO brakes!!!*

It may take ten times as long as normal to bring the car to rest, so never let yourself pick up more speed than you can definitely control.

Falling snow brings two problems:

- Grip, which becomes less reliable.

- Visibility, which can produce extra hazards and greatly increase the number and width of all your blind spots.

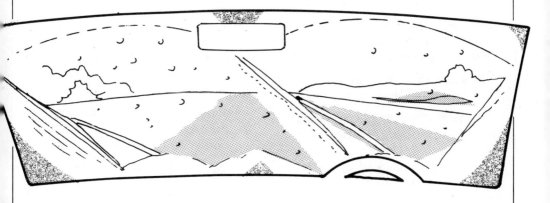

Take extra care to look out for other road users – especially those who are riding or walking with their heads tucked down and may not see you.

Always clean all your car windows free from ice and snow, as often as necessary.

If you are travelling on a motorway, it is usually best to get off it, unless lanes have been cleared especially for traffic. If this has been done – say to the two inner lanes – it is not a good idea to try to make extra headway in a snowbound 'overtaking' lane. Let someone else do the 'leading'. You should be in no hurry to arrive, only desperate to arrive *safely*.

# Fog

Of all the weather conditions which you meet on the roads, the worst is undoubtedly *fog*.

With virtually all other weather hazards, you can always find somewhere quiet and traffic-free where you can practise your skills alone – except in fog. Therefore, for you as a motorist, you must always treat fog as the worst of the weather conditions.

Given a choice, you are always safer deciding *not* to travel at all. But if it really becomes vital to drive in the fog, remember that not only will your vision be distorted, reduced and often nullified, but fog also plays havoc with sound, often making it difficult to hear other traffic or to rely on what you think you hear.

Remember that fog is often patchy. A sudden clear spell can often be replaced by a just as sudden thick 'pea souper'.

- Keep all your lights on, especially your rear fog lights.

- You will usually find that main headlights are not as effective as dipped headlights. The reason for this is that the main beam lights reflect back from the fog straight into your eyes.

- If you have fog lights fitted to the front and rear ('intensive fog lights') of the car, use them; but make sure you use your main front and rear lights as well.

- Leaving your car in fog can be hazardous, so, if possible, try to park off the road somewhere.

- Never leave it parked on the wrong side of the road.

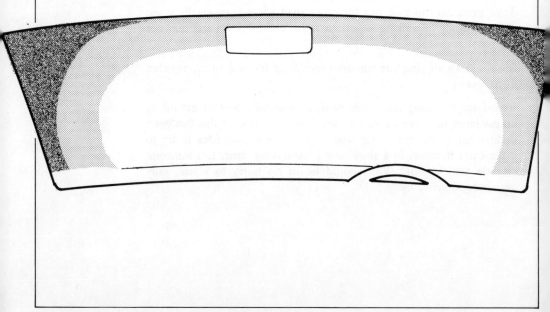

The secret of any bad weather driving is always to *anticipate the worst* and to drive within your known capabilities. If the thought of driving on ice or packed snow worries you, get some training on a 'skid pan' *before* the bad weather starts.

There is no need to be frightened of a skid pan because the beauty of learning on it is that everything happens so much slower than it does on the road – you, therefore, have plenty of time to practise and gain control.

# Driving on motorways

Motorway driving is akin to flying an aeroplane. There is no problem in doing it: most of the problems are associated with starting and finishing.

- In the air, it is taking off and landing.

- On the motorway, it is *joining* and *leaving.*

The immediate benefits of travelling on motorways are no junctions, sharp bends, roundabouts, traffic lights or any sudden changes of direction at all.

It is easier to make progress, and, provided you use your mirrors carefully and take all observations before changing lanes, it is much safer than driving on ordinary roads. Because of this, drivers tend to drive at much higher speeds – certainly higher *average* speeds. It is, therefore, most important that you are totally fit to concentrate solely on the task of driving.

### Joining a motorway

Joining a motorway is a question of knowing well in advance where you intend to go and which lane you need to follow, to join it safely.

- You can join some motorways simply by continuing along the road you are already on and checking the signs as you go.

- To join others, you will need to get on a roundabout and select the motorway exit.

At a roundabout, make sure you travel in the right direction; if you go the wrong way it might mean a forty-mile detour.

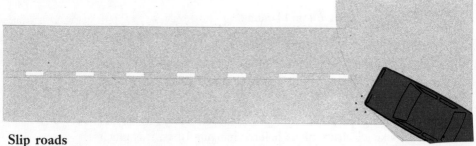

### Slip roads

As you leave the roundabout, you will join a **slip road** which leads directly – and usually only – to the motorway.

The slip road leads directly up or down to the motorway, depending upon whether the roundabout is above or below it.

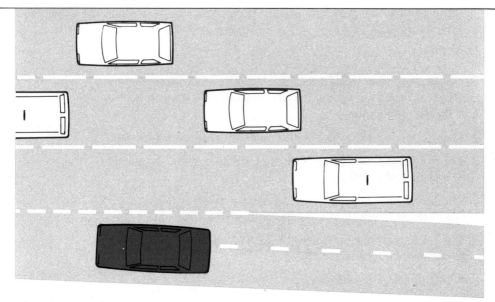

## Acceleration lane

The slip road leads into an acceleration lane, which is an extra piece of road alongside the motorway.

The purpose of the acceleration lane is to give you the opportunity to pick up your speed to the speed of the traffic already driving along the motorway. This enables you to merge in with this traffic, keeping initially to the left hand of the two or three lanes of the motorway.

Stay in the acceleration lane until you have had time to assess your speed in relation to all other traffic. Only then are you ready to change lanes and overtake other traffic.

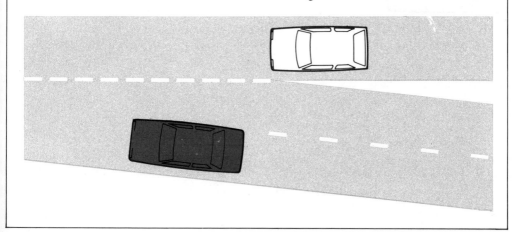

**Four time rules**

Remember that the 'two-second rule' applies even more on the motorway than normal driving. In fact, you can even think of having four separate 'time rules':

1 The two-second rule, which is the minimum distance between cars.

2 The five-second rule, which is the time/distance ahead you should be looking and planning.

3 The ten-second rule, which is the time it takes to overtake any other vehicle travelling at ten miles an hour less than you.

4 The ten-minute rule, in which you try to concentrate your driving in spells of ten minutes or less:

- making maximum headway

- then following another vehicle

- then totally relaxing

- making headway once more for perhaps ten minutes

The ten-minute rule works well for any long-distance drive and takes much tedium out of driving, particularly when you are behind the wheel for any length of time.

One of the best ways to travel on a motorway is to find someone ahead of you who is driving at the sort of pace you want, then follow him at about four to five seconds distance behind, allowing him to act as your pacemaker.

 **5 SECS.**

## Changing lanes

On motorways, you only need to change lanes if the traffic in the lane ahead of you is slower or faster than you really want to be. When you do, be absolutely certain about your MSM sequence. Before changing direction, use your centre *and* your door/wing mirrors.

- Watch the traffic coming up behind you.

- Select a suitable gap.

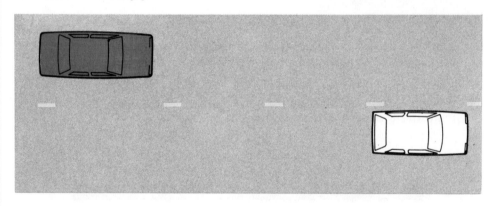

- Ensure that you only pull across after signalling.

- Make sure that you do so at the safest possible moment.

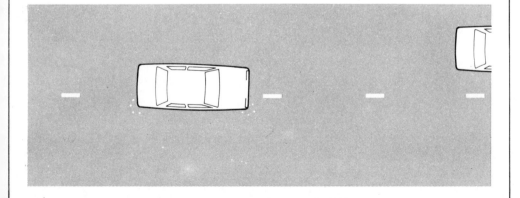

Ideally, keep in the left lane as much as you can. But if the traffic is particularly heavy, you can remain in the centre lane of three, provided:

- the traffic in the left lane is travelling much slower than you are

- your speed in the centre lane is sufficient to keep up with traffic flow in that lane

## Three important points to remember

1 Heavy goods vehicles (HGVs) cannot overtake you if you stay in the centre of three lanes.

2 You must not stay in the right-hand 'overtaking lane' any longer than is necessary to overtake.

3 Higher speeds mean that you must be much more alert to the need to brake earlier and more firmly.

*Alertness* is very much the name of the motorway game.

## Changing motorways

Sometimes you'll need to change from one motorway to another. In some circumstances, this can be done without even noticing the change.

However, quite often you'll have to pay attention to the traffic signs ahead to correctly position your car for the lane you require.

Occasionally, you'll meet some rather wide, curved 'spaghetti junction' interchanges, simply to change from one route to another.

They are all well signposted and, if you keep your head, you'll have no problems. Look for the signs and follow the lanes.

### Leaving a motorway

Leaving a motorway is no more trouble than joining one.

- Plan ahead and get into the left-hand lane early.

- Don't wait until after you've gone past the countdown markers.

- Get into the left lane by the time the first countdown marker is seen.

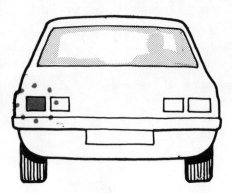

- Then, using your left indicator all the time, enter the 'deceleration lane'.

- Use your brakes to slow down sufficiently before entering the slip road.

It is important to use your brakes because you can so easily be misled about your speed while on the motorway; you only realise exactly how fast you were travelling when you arrive too soon in the normal stream of road traffic.

### The golden rule of all driving

Only drive at a speed at which you can safely stop in the distance ahead you can clearly see. This rule applies as much to motorways as anywhere.

It *doubly* applies in bad weather and at night.

- If you cannot see, don't commit yourself.

- But equally, don't just come to a grinding halt.

- What is needed is a careful selection of the safest speed for the circumstances!

# STAGE 12

# Ten panics, or, 'What do you do if . . .'

**1 Your bonnet flies open when you are driving along**

*Answer*

- Try to remember what your last view of the road ahead was like.

- Brake firmly and progressively.

- If it is a real emergency, your mirrors will tell you how safe it is to do this.

- Hold the steering wheel firmly. Do not try to steer out of the problem.

- Try to look around the front – through the front door – and get your front passenger to do the same.

**2 Your windscreen shatters**

This is not nearly so bad. It will almost certainly happen to every motorist who drives long enough.

*Answer*

- First of all, don't panic!

- Look through what is left of your screen and you'll be surprised how much you can still see.

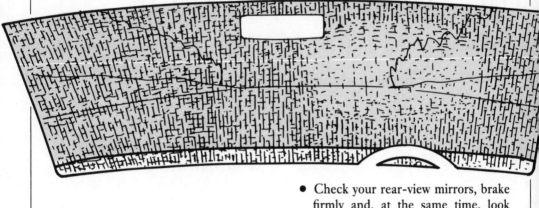

- Check your rear-view mirrors, brake firmly and, at the same time, look ahead through what vision you have for somewhere to pull off the road safely.

- Don't punch a hole in the screen with your fist. It is not necessary, and you'll spend the rest of your life having bits of glass spat at you through the heater.

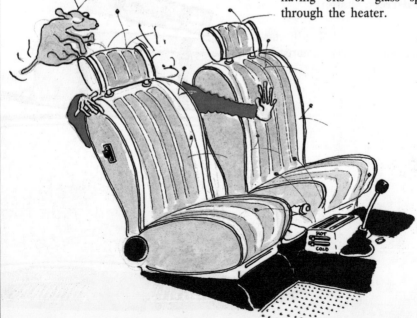

**3 Your brakes fail**

*Answer*

- Gently try to pull the handbrake on. It won't have a lot of effect and it depends upon what speed you were travelling before your brakes went.

- Decelerate and, if at all possible, get into a lower gear – progressively if you can – so that you use your lowest gears to slow you right down.

- Then use your handbrake to bring you to a stop.

- Failing all else, leave it in a low gear and switch off.

- Make sure you don't lock the steering lock.

**4 Your rear tyre bursts**

*Answer*

- Hold the steering wheel firmly, as the car will try to sway from side to side, especially at speed.

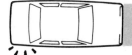

- Try to steer the safest possible course.

- Look for the safest place on the left to pull up to change the tyre.

**5 Your front tyre bursts**

*Answer*

- When this occurs, there will be a pronounced pull to the side of the deflated tyre.

- You therefore need to steer against this pull to keep going straight.

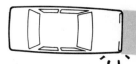

- Once more, look for the safest place to stop and change tyres.

- With burst tyres, there is no chance that you can use the tyres again, so if you drive some metres on them you'll not do any *more* damage.

- With a puncture, however, if you drive on it at all, you will normally prevent the tyres from ever being used again.

### 6 Your gear lever comes off in your hand

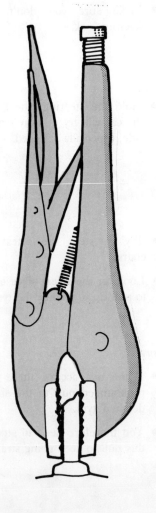

*Answer*

- Carry on driving (or coasting if you managed to do it in neutral).

- Realise that, so long as you don't actually need to select a new gear, you can drive for some distance. This is fine if it broke off at the end of a gear change, but not so good if you wanted to select a new gear and then broke it off.

- Again, you need to look for a safe place to pull in.

- If you have a 'stump' left, you can always use a mole wrench to act as a temporary gear lever.

- But if it broke off flush, you're stuck.

- The only exception is that if the car is fixed in second or third gear, it is possible to drive in that gear alone. But, unless you can do it in total safety, it is best not to.

**7 Your accelerator pedal sticks down**    *Answer*

- The one thing *not* to do is to put down the clutch or select neutral. If you do, all sorts of nasties will happen to the engine.

- Brake firmly against the engine speed.

- Find the safest place possible (e.g., the left lane of a motorway, and then on to the hard shoulder) and switch off the engine.

- Make sure you do not lock the steering lock.

**8 Your battery is flat**    *Answer*

- If *your* answer is 'What shape should it be?' join the AA/RAC or whatever.

- But if you find your car won't start and the battery gets weaker and weaker (the starter motor slows right down), or if you left your headlights on all night, disconnect the battery from the car (never charge it in situ) and put it on charge for about ten to twelve hours.

- You can jump-start the engine if you use jump leads and another car:

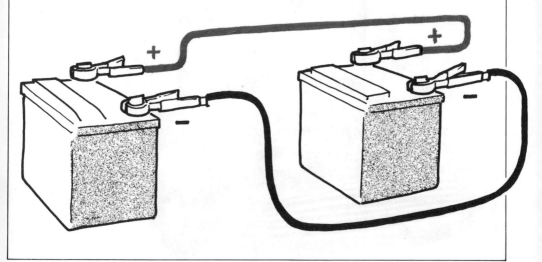

*Get the cars parallel or bonnet to bonnet.

*Switch on the good engine, connect the black lead to the dud battery and then to the good one.

*Then connect the red lead to the positive terminal of the dud battery and then to the live one.

*Keep the engine speed up and then once or twice try to start the engine of the car with the dud battery.

*If it fires, keep the engine speed up to avoid the engine dying on you.

*Then disconnect the jump leads – red first, and then the black.

### 9 Your engine overheats

*Answer*

You are driving along when you notice that the temperature gauge is climbing (or has climbed) into the red section.

- If it is summer or the weather is warm, you need to decide if it is likely to be caused by sitting in a long queue of traffic or by losing water through a leaking hose or radiator.

*If the former, a reasonably fast drive will cure it.

*If the latter, you will need to pull off the road in order to replace the hose when it is cool, and then to refill the radiator.

- If it happens in winter or cold weather, you might be able to keep on driving even though you only have a little bit of water in the radiator.

- But you will need to keep an eye on the gauge as you continue to drive and may even need to stop at intervals.

**Warning** Never, ever remove the radiator cap while the water is hot. It is not just hot, it is superheated steam and could burn you quite severely.

**10 Your headlights fail as you are driving along**

*Answer*

- Pull in off the road.

- Try your emergency flashers; if they work, you know your battery is OK.

- If it is only a fuse, keep your emergency flashers going and also any interior lights you have (including torches) to make sure you are seen by oncoming traffic.

With all of the above ten panics, if you have to pull off the road or if you break down on the hard shoulder of a motorway, do not let your passengers or yourself stay in the car if there is any possibility at all of being hit. Get them out and keep them safe.

You can always sweep up the bits of your car afterwards ... but not if you were inside the car when it was hit.

# STAGE 13
# Drinking, drugs and driving

## Drinking and driving

There is only one moral law about drinking alcohol and driving a motor car – **don't**.

But we do live in a real world, and rather than have to force a total prohibition on the consumption of alcohol by drivers, we should regard the alcohol content in our blood as the guideline.

- For several years now, eighty milligrams of alcohol per 100 millilitres of blood has been the yardstick. Although this has been re-rated recently, the basic principle still exists.

- One or two drinks is anyone's maximum.

If you want to be clever, you can actually buy 'mock breath testing kits', which will tell you when you are over the limit. I remember testing myself during and after a dinner. Sherry, followed by a few glasses of my 'house white' and finally a port kept me still under the limit. Then a final touch of class with a liqueur threw me right over the top.

The real answer, of course, is never to mix alcohol and driving.

One of the greatest perils of alcohol is the feeling of euphoria which it gives you and the belief that everything you do is perfect. It is this false sense of security which is the most dangerous aspect of all.

A driver who has had two or three drinks but feels that he is absolutely safe and under full control is the one who will take those very risks which can kill. You must also not believe that, because you have not yet drunk enough to pass the limit, you are safe from being guilty of driving under the influence. The law still allows prosecutions to be made against drivers who have passed the breath test but are guilty under Section 5 or 6 of the Road Traffic Act, 1972.

- Section 5 refers to offences related to the consumption of alcohol while you are

  *driving

  *attempting to drive

  *in charge of a motor vehicle on a road or in a public place

  The only evidence required to convict you can be that of witnesses, medical opinion, specimen analysis, or refusal to provide a specimen without a legitimate excuse.

- Under Section 6, the prescribed limits of alcohol in the body are

  *blood: 80 milligrammes of alcohol per 100 millilitres

  *breath: 35 microgrammes per 100 millilitres

  *urine: 107 milligrammes per 100 millilitres

In law, the only defence for refusing to provide a specimen is that there was no likelihood at all of you driving the car while under the influence of alcohol. That is why you can be convicted for having too much to drink, pulling off the road to sleep it off and keeping the keys in your pocket.

The Scandinavians have a better solution. If they want to go out drinking they hand in their car keys at the local police station.

Learning to drive will probably cost you between £250 and £500. The extra cost of a taxi home is negligible in comparison. And the *value* of your driving licence once you have it must run into thousands of pounds. So don't lose it for the price of a taxi, or getting a friend to stay sober. It is not just the cost of losing your licence – you could find yourself in prison. And you might easily find yourself guilty of the manslaughter of friends, family or a complete stranger.

The problem is that, because drinking tends to be a sociable habit, you often need your vehicle to indulge. The solution is to ensure that one or more members of your party does not drink and acts as chauffeur to the rest. You can then either do this on a rotation basis, or suitably reimburse the kindness of the person who does it willingly.

Over the years, drinking and driving has not been classified as a crime in the same category as burglary. But recently, considerable pressure has been mounted to change this line of thinking. The law allows any police officer to stop any driver whom he thinks *might* have committed any moving traffic offence. Having stopped him, he can ask him to take a breath test (if the officer thinks he has had a drink or two).

Police officers already have the option to breath test any driver they want to test, but for many years the pressures on them to do so have been minimal. But this has changed. Drinking and driving is now as unsocial as burglary, and the results are far more devastating. Losing your licence is automatic, and getting it back again in six or twelve months' time doesn't solve the problem of paying astronomical rates for insurance.

# Drugs and driving

The effects of drugs on your driving capabilities is an issue you need to examine carefully. Even taking an aspirin or paracetamol will slow down your reactions and cause your driving to be more lethargic. One simple rule to use with regard to health and driving is: 'One degree under? Five miles per hour slower!'

If you are feeling under par

- you will react slower

- you will find you miss opportunities

- you will fail to recognise warning signs early enough to take effective action

You need to drive more cautiously and with a greater effort of concentration to keep alert.

This applies just as much when you have taken any form of drug, even those whose sole purpose is to reduce pain. They may cut down on the amount of pain you suffer, but they will do nothing to improve your traffic awareness.

It is a fact that women have more accidents during their pre-menstrual countdown than at any other time.

If you cannot give your full attention to road and traffic conditions, your concentration and ability to avoid accidents are under greater stress.

There is one exception to this rule about the use of drugs and driving. It applies to those people who have to take drugs or medication prescribed by their doctors so that they can continue with a normal life, such as insulin for diabetic drivers. As long as they continue to take their drugs, they are perfectly all right. It is only when they stop taking them that trouble may start.

In all cases of medicines prescribed by a doctor, make sure you find out what effect they may have on your driving. 'Cough cures', for example, often contain warnings advising you not to operate heavy machinery while taking the medicine. A car is a heavy machine, so don't mix the two!

If you are ill enough to need medicine, you are ill enough to stay at home. If you have to travel, use public transport or take a taxi.

**Remember:** you can lose your driving licence just as easily for being under the influence of 'drugs' as you can for alcohol.

# INDEX